FORERUNNERS: IDEAS FIRST FROM THE UNIVERSITY OF
MINNESOTA PRESS

Original e-works to spark new scholarship

FORERUNNERS: IDEAS FIRST is a thought-in-process series of
breakthrough digital works. Written between fresh ideas and finished
books, Forerunners draws on scholarly work initiated in notable
blogs, social media, conference plenaries, journal articles, and the
synergy of academic exchange. This is gray literature publishing:
where intense thinking, change, and speculation take place in
scholarship.

The Politics of Bitcoin

The Politics of Bitcoin
Software as Right-Wing Extremism

David Golumbia

University of Minnesota Press

MINNEAPOLIS

Published by the University of Minnesota Press, 2016
111 Third Avenue South, Suite 290
Minneapolis, MN 55401–2520
http://www.upress.umn.edu

The University of Minnesota is an equal-opportunity educator and employer.

Contents

1. Bitcoin, Digital Culture, and Right-Wing Politics

IN THE EARLY 2010S, and then especially throughout 2013, observers of digital culture began to read more and more about a new form of digital payment called Bitcoin. Although any number of digital payment systems had already emerged—from relatively straightforward tools for money transfer such as new Western Union services, online bill paying, and PayPal, to more exotic systems such as Liberty Reserve (Langlois 2013), "beenz" (Richardson 2001), and forms of "digital gold" like E-Gold (Zetter 2009)—Bitcoin was said to be different. Its difference stemmed from at least two sources: first, that it was based on a relatively new form of cryptographic software technology called a "blockchain," and second, that throughout 2013 Bitcoin had skyrocketed in its value relative to official world currencies like the U.S. dollar. At the end of 2012 one could buy a single Bitcoin for around US$13. By May 2013, that one Bitcoin was worth upward of US$100, nearly an 800 percent gain for those fortunate enough to have held it for five months. In November and December of 2013 Bitcoin's value briefly exceeded US$1,200 ("History of Bitcoin"). In just under a year investors who timed their buying and selling correctly could have made around 8,000 percent in profits, far exceeding the performance of most, perhaps even all, traditional investments. Those who had bought or "mined" Bitcoin earlier in its existence (the first coins were created in 2009 and started out as essentially worthless) could and well may have realized gains that dwarf even these. This remarkable performance thrust Bitcoin into the public eye, eventually attracting numerous start-up projects, venture capitalists, and investors.

By far the majority of interest in Bitcoin came from technologists and those who follow and admire the work of technologists. To those of us who were watching Bitcoin with an eye toward politics and economics, though, something far more striking than Bitcoin's explosive rise in value became apparent: in the name of this new technology, extremist ideas were gaining far more traction than they previously had outside of the extremist literature to which they had largely been confined. Dogma propagated almost exclusively by far-right groups like the Liberty League, the John Birch Society, the militia movement, and the Tea Party, conspiracy theorists like Alex Jones and David Icke, and to a lesser extent rightist outlets like the Fox media group and some right-wing politicians, was now being repeated by many who seemed not to know the origin of the ideas, or the functions of those ideas in contemporary politics.

These ideas are not simply heterodox or contrarian: they are pieces of a holistic worldview that has been deliberately developed and promulgated by right-wing ideologues. To anyone aware of the history of right-wing thought in the United States and Europe, they are shockingly familiar: that central banking such as that practiced by the U.S. Federal Reserve is a deliberate plot to "steal value" from the people to whom it actually belongs; that the world monetary system is on the verge of imminent collapse due to central banking policies, especially fractional reserve banking; that "hard" currencies such as gold provide meaningful protection against that purported collapse; that inflation is a plot to steal money from the masses and hand it over to a shadowy cabal of "elites" who operate behind the scenes; and more generally that the governmental and corporate leaders and wealthy individuals we all know are "controlled" by those same "elites."

Understanding how Bitcoin comes to embody these extremist ideas requires situating it within two broader analytical frameworks. The first of these is the phenomenon that scholars call *cyberlibertarianism*. The central texts describing cyberlibertarianism are Barbrook and Cameron (1996) and Winner (1997); for more recent accounts see Turner (2008) as well as Golumbia (2013b, 2013c, in preparation). In its most basic and limited form, cyberlibertarianism is sometimes summarized as the principle that "governments should not regulate the internet" (Malcolm 2013). This belief was articulated with particular force in the 1996 "Declaration of the Independence of Cyberspace" written by the libertarian activist, Grateful Dead lyricist, and Electronic Frontier Foundation founder (EFF is a leading "digital rights" and technology industry advocacy organization) John Perry Barlow, which declared that "governments of the industrial world" are "not welcome" in and "have no sovereignty" over the digital realm.

In practice, opposition to "government regulation of the internet" is best understood as a core (and in important ways vague) tenet, around which circulate greater and greater claims for the "freedom" created by digital technology. At its most expansive, cyberlibertarianism can be thought of as something like a belief according to which *freedom will emerge inherently from the increasing development of digital technology,* and therefore entails that efforts to interfere with or regulate that

3

development must be antithetical to freedom—although what "freedom" means in this context is much less clear than it may seem. As Winner (1997, 14–15) puts it, to be a cyberlibertarian is to believe that "the dynamism of digital technology is our true destiny. There is no time to pause, reflect or ask for more influence in shaping these developments. . . . In the writings of cyberlibertarians those able to rise to the challenge are the champions of the coming millennium. The rest are fated to languish in the dust."

Cyberlibertarianism is thus not to be understood as the belief system of someone who overtly describes themselves as a *political* libertarian—a member of a libertarian party or someone who votes for libertarian candidates—and who supports or promotes the development of digital technology. Someone who fits this description would likely have cyberlibertarian beliefs, of course (and a few pundits associated with the Koch brothers–funded Mercatus Center do explicitly embrace the label; see Thierer and Szoka 2009). But the analysis of cyberlibertarianism is getting at something subtler: the way that a set of slogans and beliefs associated with the spread of digital technology incorporate critical parts of a right-wing worldview even as they manifest a surface rhetorical commitment to values that do not immediately appear to come from the right.

Certainly, many leaders in the digital technology industries, and quite a few leaders who do not work for corporations, openly declare their adherence to libertarian or other right-wing ideologies. Just a brief list of these includes figures like Elon Musk, Peter Thiel, Eric Raymond, Jimmy Wales, Eric Schmidt, and Travis Kalanick. Furthermore, the number of leaders who demur from such political points of view is small, and their demurrals are often shallow. But the group of people whose beliefs deserve to be labeled "cyberlibertarian" is much larger than this. The core tenet of cyberlibertarianism—the insistence that "governments should not regulate the internet"—appears to be compatible with a wide range of political viewpoints. As EFF's senior global policy analyst Jeremy Malcolm (2013) has written, "Even politically progressive activists are inclined to be more distrustful of governmental intervention online than offline, in an expression of Internet exceptionalism."

As Winner makes clear in his 1997 paper, the critical point about cyberlibertarianism as a belief system is that it "links ecstatic enthusiasm for electronically mediated forms of living with radical, right-wing libertarian ideas about the proper definition of freedom, social life, economics, and politics" (14). His emphasis on "proper" definition is the key to Winner's analysis: people who subscribe to cyberlibertarianism for the most part do not describe themselves as cyberlibertarians and may not call themselves "libertarians" or even identify with right-wing political parties. Instead, and at least sometimes without explicitly knowing it, they accept definitions of certain fundamental terms that come from the political right, especially when digital technologies are at issue.

The most important of these redefined terms that occur repeatedly in discussions of Bitcoin are "freedom" and "government," both of which are central to all cyberlibertarian and political libertarian rhetoric. Referring to the 1994 manifesto "Cyberspace and the American Dream: A Magna Carta for the Knowledge Age" by Esther Dyson, George Gilder, George Keyworth, and Alvin Toffler, Winner (1997, 16) writes:

> Characteristic of this way of thinking is a tendency to conflate the activities of freedom-seeking individuals with the operations of enormous, profit-seeking business firms. In the "Magna Carta for the Knowledge Age," concepts of rights, freedoms, access, and ownership justified as appropriate to individuals are marshaled to support the machinations of enormous transnational firms. We must recognize, the manifesto argues, that "Government does not

own cyberspace, the people do." One might read this as a suggestion that cyberspace is a commons in which people have shared rights and responsibilities. But that is definitely not where the writers carry their reasoning.

The "freedom" these writers advocate turns out, in a way they themselves do not always acknowledge, to be identical with the use of "free" in the phrase "free market": that is, free from government regulation. Building on the foundational, often unspoken rightist beliefs about the uniquely oppressive nature of governmental power, they "advocate greater concentrations of power over the conduits of information which they are confident will create an abundance of cheap, socially available bandwidth. Today developments of this kind are visible in the corporate mergers that have produced a tremendous concentration of control over not only the conduits of cyberspace but the content it carries" (16). Indeed, in the nearly two decades since Winner wrote, this is exactly what we have seen happen; in the name of vague slogans like "internet freedom" (Powers and Jablonski 2015), wealth and power have concentrated enormously (Hardoon 2015; Piketty 2014) as digital technology has spread all around the globe.

From a cyberlibertarian perspective, governments—*all* governments, not simply whatever current "bad" government we describe as doing wrong—exist *only* to curtail the freedom that is inherently negative (in the classic sense of "negative" vs. "positive" freedoms developed in Berlin 1958): to be "free" simply *is* to be "free" from government. The core cyberlibertarian belief that "governments should not regulate the internet" really makes sense only if it is true that government exists to curtail rather than to promote human freedom. Yet in most non-rightist political theory, government exists in no small part to *promote* human freedom.

Their advocates make it sound like, and may often believe that, cyberlibertarian commitments are about *limiting* power, but this is only true so long as we construe "government" as equivalent with "power," and "the internet" as being oppositional to power, rather than, at least in significant part, being strongly aligned with it. The most direct way to arrive at this perspective is to accept the definition of government developed by the far right, especially anarcho-capitalist theorists like Murray Rothbard and David Friedman, and echoed by politicians like Ronald Reagan and Margaret Thatcher. According to this view, "government" is *inherently* totalitarian and tyrannical; indeed, "government" and "tyranny" are essentially synonyms.

Cyberlibertarian doctrine did not develop in a vacuum. It fits into, and at best does nothing to resist, the profound rightward drift evident in so much of contemporary politics. This becomes clear when we examine the explicit political and economic doctrine and practice that is usually called *libertarianism* in the United States (here meaning the political movement that is explicitly advocated by right-wing partisan institutions such as the Cato Institute, the Heartland Foundation, the Mises Institute, and others, as well as astroturf movements like the Tea Party and political figures like Ron Paul and Rand Paul) and its connections with the less explicit doctrine analysts call *neoliberalism*. Both of these doctrines or dogmas stem from the writings of core right-wing thinkers such as Friedrich August von Hayek, Ludwig von Mises, Milton Friedman, Rothbard, and others, as well as their more recent followers. The most trenchant critic of this work, on whose research my analysis relies in particular, is the economic historian and theorist Philip Mirowski, whose *Never Let a Serious Crisis Go to Waste* (2014) remains the single most comprehensive account of what he calls the Neoliberal Thought Collective and the nearly identical Mont Pelerin Society (MPS), of which Hayek was the founding president.

Mirowski, along with some of his colleagues, has explained with particular cogency how Hayek and others disseminated neoliberal doctrine. From somewhat different angles, writers like Chip Berlet (2009), Berlet along with Matthew Lyons (2000), Claire Conner (2013), Sara Diamond (1995), Michael Perelman (2007), Jill Lepore (2010), and the writers in Flanders's edited volume (2010) give us thoroughly documented accounts of how those wider spheres of right-wing political thought and practice operate, distributed among actors whose overt adherence to MPS doctrine can vary widely, though they tend to be found far more on the right than the left.

The journalist Mark Ames explains how apparently disparate political interests, especially in the context of Silicon Valley, can be seen to work together. Reflecting on some surprising alliances between today's technology giants and the lobbying groups and of the world's major extractive resource companies, Ames (2015) writes that

> even if we still give Google and Facebook the benefit of the doubt, and allow that their investments in the Cato Institute and the Competitive Enterprise Institute weren't directly motivated by killing Obamacare and throwing millions of struggling Americans back into the ranks of the uninsured and prematurely dying—nevertheless, they are accessories, and very consciously so. Big Tech's larger political goals are in alignment with the old extraction industry's: undermining the countervailing power of government and public politics to weaken its ability to impede their growing dominance over their portions of the economy, and to tax their obscene stores of cash.
>
> Google—like Facebook, like Koch Industries—wants a government that's strong enough to enforce its dominant private power over the economy and citizens and protect its wealth, but too broken and too alienated from the public to adequately represent the public interest against their domineering monopolistic power.

In this way, much right-wing discourse, even when it appears to be focused on issues that are not purely economic, turns out to work extremely well for the most concentrated sources of capital and power in our world.

Power is one of the central subjects for political analysis, and perhaps *the* central subject: who has power, who wants power, what the perspectives those who have and want power are on the creation and maintenance of methods for the management of power. We might say that right-wing politics sides emotionally and practically with power—it identifies with power, and via this identification works to ensure that nobody interferes with the concentration and exercise of power. On this view, left-wing politics is specifically focused on the limitation of power, on mechanisms for distributing power equitably, and on the excesses that almost inevitably emerge when power is allowed to grow unchecked.

Rather than a balance of powers and regular elections to curb the inherent possibility of abuse of power, the cypherpunks and crypto-anarchists accept, often without appearing even to realize it, the far-right, libertarian/anarcho-capitalist definition of government that extends from the German social theorist Max Weber (who famously and tendentiously defined the state as a "monopoly of the legitimate use of physical force within a given territory"; see Weber 1919, 33; see also Giddens 1985 for a thorough critique of Weber's definition) to Ronald Reagan's inaugural address of 1981, in which he famously claimed that "government is not the solution to our problem; government is the problem." In *Why Government Is the Problem* (1993), Milton Friedman, a key player in the creation of neoliberal economic doctrine, makes the same case at greater length.

The clearest articulation of these views is found in the work of arch right-wing thinker and Cato Foundation cofounder Murray Rothbard. In an essay titled "Anatomy of the State," first published in the 1974 volume *Egalitarianism as a Revolt against Nature,* Rothbard abruptly dismisses with almost the entirety of political theory prior to Hayek, while taking Hayek even farther than he was willing to go, at least in print. Arguably the position Rothbard develops is among the farthest to the political right offered in Western discourse, with the exception of those who explicitly identify with fascism: "We must, therefore, emphasize that 'we' are not the government; the government is not 'us.' The government does not in any accurate sense 'represent' the majority of the people" (Rothbard 1974, 56). With no supporting argument or analysis, Rothbard dismisses nearly all the political theory on which democratic rules are based (even the monarchist Thomas Hobbes thought that the sovereign represented the people over whom he ruled, in an abstract sense) and the entire theory of representative democracy.

At their limit—a limit that is often surpassed in current cypherpunk and crypto-anarchist rhetoric and practice—these views suggest bizarrely that only government is *capable* of violence, and that even when private institutions and enterprises engage in what appears to be physical violence, it is in some sense of a different order than that practiced by governments. Even more bizarrely, these views entail that democratic government lies about the one thing that does in fact distinguish it from other forms of power—that it is directly accountable for its actions to the people from whom it draws its power—while simultaneously entailing that power derived from capital and markets *is* accountable to citizens. Worse still, it suggests that this market-based form of accountability does not merely trump the electoral and legal accountability built into representative government, but also shields corporate forces from the political critique to which the right routinely subjects government. In other words, no matter how much power corporations take, their power can never be "evil" in the way that governmental power inherently is.

There are certain keywords that move with a fair amount of ease between explicit right-wing discourse and more general political discussion but that serve as rallying cries for right-wing political action. Two of the most prominent and most relevant to Bitcoin are "tyranny" and "liberty." When the right wing uses them, these words are removed from their more general meanings and grafted onto holistic bodies of political thought, so that it can sound reasonable to oppose Social Security or Medicare on the grounds that they offend "liberty" and constitute "tyranny," despite the signal lack of substantive political thought that would make such assessments coherent. It is no accident that the right-wing ideologue and talk show host Mark Levin titles one of his best-selling books *Liberty and Tyranny: A Conservative Manifesto* (2009), or that he misleadingly claims that "the Founders understood that the greatest threat to liberty is an all-powerful central government" (4), and that "conservatism is the antidote to tyranny" (11), a "tyranny" that in the United States is best exemplified to Levin by social programs enacted under the New Deal (6–7). Despite our abhorrence of real tyranny, then, the right wing uses the words "liberty" and "tyranny" to solicit and activate populist energy *against* exactly those democratically enacted structures and programs among whose main purposes is to curtail the tyrannical abuse of individual liberty by concentrated economic power (Puddington 2013 describes this dynamic with regard to uses of the word "tyranny" by the Tea Party). The effect is to make such concentrations of power even more possible and even less subject to oversight, and this is very much the direction in which Bitcoin heads.

There are many things worth saying about Bitcoin. This short book is concerned not with providing a thorough description of the technology, a detailed history of its uses, an account of the scandals and triumphs associated with it, or profiles of the various personalities involved in its creation and subsequent use (for which good introductory resources include Lanchester 2016; Murray 2013; Pagliery 2014; Payne 2013; Popper 2015; Robinson 2014; Scott 2016). Its goal is more limited: to show how much of the economic and political thought on which Bitcoin is based emerges directly from ideas that travel the gamut from the sometimes-extreme Chicago School economics of Milton Friedman to the explicit extremism of Federal Reserve conspiracy theorists. While it is beyond doubt that many who "believe" in Bitcoin think they do not subscribe to these theories, it frequently turns out that they rely on assumptions and concepts that do emerge from the far right. As they are currently configured, Bitcoin and the blockchain technology on which it rests satisfy needs that make sense only in the context of right-wing politics; those of us who do not share those politics must, therefore, view Bitcoin and the blockchain with both skepticism and a clear eye for the political terms and concepts invoked in the discourse surrounding them.

I am sometimes asked to account for Bitcoin enthusiasm among those with explicitly left-wing politics. My response is to ask two questions analytically prior to this one: first, to ask for accounts of where and how it happened that a technology developed specifically to magnify the powers favored by the political right has mutated so as not to serve those powers but the forces they oppose; and second, to ask for accounts on economic and political-economic grounds that proceed from left-wing thought (whether Marxian or Keynesian) to the need for and utility of Bitcoin. Almost uniformly, responses to these queries repeat some of the rightist tropes about central banking and governmental tyranny I describe here, and those that do not (e.g., Bauwens 2014) emerge very skeptical about Bitcoin. Perhaps Bitcoin and the blockchain can serve politics other than the ones from which they were birthed and which they continue to embody; my goal here is to document those politics and to show what any non-rightist politics of Bitcoin needs to overcome.

2. Central Banking, Inflation, and Right-Wing Extremism

IN THE 1960S AND 1970S the John Birch Society (JBS) was the best-known exponent of right-wing extremist thought in the United States. JBS founder Robert Welch's 1966 essay "The Truth in Time," which appeared in the JBS house organ *American Opinion,* remains a central text for U.S. right-wing extremism. Obsessed, as the right was at that time, with the "menace of the Communist conspiracy" which is nonetheless "only a tool of the total conspiracy," Welch's propaganda is directed at a "ruling clique" called "the Insiders." "Under the guise of humanitarianism, and in the pretended promotion of freedom and brotherhood," Welch writes, "these *Insiders,* and the gullible idealists who served as their dupes, were busily undermining the very beliefs and institutions which made the Nineteenth Century a high water mark of such civilization as man has laboriously achieved."

According to Welch and the JBS, the main tool of these "Insiders" was "progressive legislation"; on this view all social welfare programs, such as worker's compensation and Medicare, "made possible, of course, by idealists with only the noblest of intentions," were "rot introduced in the name of progress." The goal of such measures was to "reduce the responsibilities and rights of individual citizens, while steadily increasing the quantity, the reach, and the potential tyranny of governments." And chief among the tools to accomplish these goals were "such decisively important measures as . . . central banking, a graduated personal income tax, and the direct election of senators."

By "central banking" Welch refers in particular to the U.S. Federal Reserve, the body that has remained a touchstone for the far right in the United States since its creation by the Federal Reserve Act of 1913. Welch writes that the Fed's

> long-range significance and use could be well hidden under the pretended objectives at the time of its founding. And its ultimate value to the conspirators could be tremendously enhanced by the character and ability of the good men drawn into its top positions during the early decades of its existence. But what this function and prestige of the Federal Reserve System would inevitably come to mean, in time and in actual practice, was the control of credit, the control of the money supply, the ability to spend with increasing profligacy, and the means to steal continuously from the people by the debasement of our currency, on the part of the Federal Government.

Welch insists that inflation itself is a "tax," so that, as a 2009 JBS pamphlet called "What Is Money?" puts it, "the value of money ends up in the possession of whoever does the inflating." Rather than the standard economic definition of inflation as an increase in prices, the JBS defines inflation as "an increase in the amount of currency in circulation," despite the fact that inflation frequently does occur without any such increase (see Frisch 1983 for a comprehensive discussion); inflation can have many causes, of which the printing of money is only one. Yet because, according to the JBS, the Fed has been uniquely granted the power to print money in the United States (though the Fed does not actually have the power to print money; see Federal Reserve Bank of St. Louis 2015b), it is not merely the source but the *beneficiary* of inflation, and by "expanding the money supply . . . [it] devalues the money already in circulation" (5); thus, and this claim will be key in what follows, "since the establishment of the Federal Reserve, the U.S. dollar has lost over 95% of its purchasing power while the Fed maintains a monopoly over the issuance of bank notes or cash" (4).

This description radically misstates economic principles in several important ways. Most economists feel that moderate (but not runaway) inflation *benefits* an economy, particularly by encouraging the production of goods, since they may eventually sell for more than the producer would have been able to receive simply by holding on to his or her money (the reverse of this dynamic is the main argument against deflation; see Burdekin and Siklos 2004; Frisch 1983). The comparison of the value of US$1 between 1913 and 2009 is extremely deceptive, because it fails to take into account critical factors such as wage rates, the interest rate on savings, and the possibility of investing that US$1 in capital markets or in industry. A much less conspiratorial take on economic history would point out that US$1 invested in something as simple as a bank savings account using compound interest will typically be worth much more than the simple rate of inflation would provide by 2009; even slightly more aggressive investment would produce even more gains. A far more reasonable form of comparison would be to ask whether the average laborer needs to work more or fewer hours to purchase a like good in two different circumstances— for example a quart of milk or a pound of flour. This is why economists calculate such statistics not in raw numbers but in *inflation-adjusted* terms: the point is that all prices in an economy tend to adjust with inflation, including labor. Labor that earned US$1 in 1913 is likely to have earned around US$21.67 in 2009; and US$21.67 in 2009 buys about what US$1 did in 1913.[1] This is no disaster, "hidden tax," or "destruction of value"; but viewed in isolation and taken out of context, it can provide a completely distorted view of both labor and economic history. The idea that inflation is a "destruction of value" and that the U.S. dollar has lost most or all of its purchasing power over the course of a hundred years has long been a staple of conspiracy theories, in no small part used by demagogues like Alex Jones to drive the unsuspecting toward purchases of gold and other precious metals (on inflation conspiracy theories in general see Aziz 2014 and Krugman 2011; for Ron Paul's use of inflation conspiracy theories see Foxman 2012).

The extremist characterization of inflation may have found its way into some parts of popular discourse via its promulgation in JBS and other right-wing propaganda, but it was a theory developed and cultivated by the architects of neoliberal doctrine associated with the Chicago School of economics and the Mont Pelerin Society. Chief among these was MPS founding member and early 1970s president and University of Chicago economics professor Milton Friedman. Since at least the 1950s Friedman preached a very specific point of view about inflation, summarized in his famous (Friedman 1963) dictum that "inflation is always and everywhere a monetary phenomenon." While this matter may have seemed an arcane and technical matter for economists, it ended up underwriting a new form of right-wing practice, where instead of demanding that governments take a "hands-off" policy toward markets as had their predecessors, neoliberals wanted to take control of state power

1. Statistics calculated using the U.S. Bureau of Labor Statistics Inflation Calculator, available at http://www.bls.gov/data/.

for their own ends: "A primary ambition of the neoliberal project is to redefine the shape and functions of the state, not to destroy it" (Mirowski 2014, 56). When Friedman was hired as a senior adviser to U.S. president Ronald Reagan in 1981, he thus became the chief architect of a program called *monetarism,* according to which continuous modulation of the money supply controls inflation. Thus Friedman could want "to abolish the Fed" while writing "many pages on how the Fed, if it does exist, should be run" (Doherty 1995).

Friedman's redefinition of inflation started out, like many extreme right-wing political dicta do in our time, as a fringe theory that few took seriously; then it became a backstop against which more mainstream economic theories could rest; then, via the direct exercise of the state power neoliberal theory claims to eschew, it forcibly took over the mainstream when only lukewarm resistance was offered by non-right-wing thinkers. Friedman's dogma hangs on in the right despite the fact that most non-far-right theories either posit multiple causes of inflation (Frisch 1983; Mishkin 1984) or at best suggest that "the conclusion that inflation is a monetary phenomenon does not settle the issue of what causes inflation because we also need to understand why inflationary monetary policy occurs" (Mishkin 1984, 3). Recent empirical studies (see Aziz 2013 and the discussion accompanying it; Tutino and Zarazaga 2014) dispute even the factual basis for Friedman's claims. In a famous 2007 summary of Freidman's life and work, Paul Krugman wrote that "some of the things Friedman said about 'money' and monetary policy—unlike what he said about consumption and inflation—appear to have been misleading, and perhaps deliberately so." This is not to say that Friedman's theory is itself wholly extremist ideology without the possibility of being correct, but it was long considered extreme, continues to be thought extreme by many who do not share Friedman's neoliberal politics, and today functions as a critical leg on which the ideology of neoliberal politics stands (Mirowski 2014 explains this in detail). Krugman and Mirowski suggest that Friedman's theory may have been advanced as much for the political program it helps to promote as for its influence as economic policy. We can see this effect in much Bitcoin discourse, which takes up the simplistic far-right version of Friedman's contention, claiming that inflation is just another name for the "printing of money" by central banks. From the farthest reaches of the explicitly anarcho-capitalist fringe (e.g., Frisby 2014) to the supposedly responsible mainstream (e.g., Vigna and Casey 2015, by two senior *Wall Street Journal* writers; Pagliery 2014, by a *CNNMoney* reporter), we find the same insistence on the monetary nature of inflation and the concomitant immunity of Bitcoin to inflation due to its limited total supply.

The proximate source for current Federal Reserve conspiracy theories is found in the writings of Eustace Mullins, one of the most prominent and extreme conspiracy theorists in the United States in the twentieth century, and author of the 1952 book *The Secrets of the Federal Reserve*. Mullins, a Holocaust denier and vitriolic anti-Semite, learned of the Federal Reserve during one of his visits to Ezra Pound at St. Elizabeth's Hospital in Washington, D.C., where Pound was placed in lieu of criminal prosecution for treason due to his fascist World War II radio broadcasts. Mullins (1993, 6) calls him a "political prisoner." The association between racist populism and conspiratorial opposition to the Federal Reserve is no accident: they have been intertwined at least since the Fed was created. Berlet and Lyons (2000, 194) trace these origins back even further, at least to the demonetization of silver in 1873, supposedly orchestrated by a "cabal of English, Jewish, and Wall Street bankers"; in some ways it goes back to the founding of the republic (see, e.g., Brands 2006; Michaels 1988).

The "secret" of the Federal Reserve, to Mullins, is remarkably similar to the "secret" behind the dissolution of the gold standard: it was a deliberate effort to deprive "ordinary people" (in fact, only those wealthy enough to have substantial assets in precious metals) of the value of their property, by other wealthy people who work in shadowy ways behind the scenes. The main architects of this plan are the Rothschild family, who by dint of being both British and Jewish galvanize the nationalist and racist impulses of U.S. populists:

> The most powerful men in the United States were themselves answerable to another power, a foreign power, and a power which had been steadfastly seeking to extend its control over the young republic of the United States since its very inception. This power was the financial power of England, centered in the London Branch of the House of Rothschild. The fact was that in 1910, the United States was for all practical purposes being ruled from England, and so it is today. The ten largest bank holding companies in the United States are firmly in the hands of certain banking houses, all of which have branches in London. They are J.P. Morgan Company, Brown Brothers Harriman, Warburg, Kuhn Loeb, and J. Henry Schroder. All of them maintain close relationships with the House of Rothschild, principally through the Rothschild control of international money markets through its manipulation of the price of gold. (Mullins 1993, 62–63)

It is hard not to note that despite the Federal Reserve being the ostensible target of Mullins's ire, the Fed quickly becomes for him almost indistinguishable from the targets of his other conspiracy theories, according to which the Rothschilds are the Jews are the Illuminati who have secretly controlled the United States from its inception and continue to do so to this day (in other works these connections are explicit; see, e.g., Mullins 1992).

Revising *Secrets of the Federal Reserve* in 1993 and adding the subtitle "The London Connection," Mullins makes clear that this one family continues to be responsible for orchestrating the U.S. financial system: "The controlling stock in the Federal Reserve Bank of New York, which sets the rate and scale of operations for the entire Federal Reserve System is heavily influenced by banks directly controlled by 'The London Connection,' that is, the Rothschild-controlled Bank of England" (203). This same line of thought is found in nearly identical form in the conspiratorial propaganda produced today by the Patriot, militia, and Tea Party movements in the United States (Flanders 2010; Lepore 2010; Skocpol and Williamson 2013), and by prominent conspiratorialists like Alex Jones, Henry Makow, and David Icke. In addition to Mullins, this view is promulgated in the writings of Martin Larson (1975), A. Ralph Epperson (1985), G. Edward Griffin (whose 1998 *Creature from Jekyll Island* includes an approving blurb from Ron Paul), and Murray Rothbard (2002) himself—as well as writers like Ellen Hodgson Brown (2008), who presents analyses nearly identical to those of Mullins and others without some of their explicitly rightwing trappings; and Anthony Sutton, a wide-ranging conspiratorialist whose work mixes well-documented history with elaborate speculation, and whose writings on finance and the Federal Reserve (especially Sutton 1995) repeat many of the same "facts" and inferences found in Mullins and others.

Bitcoin enthusiasts repackage material from these writers almost verbatim, regardless of whether they know the origins of that material. Despite the general rightist orientation of much digital culture, central bank conspiracism is relatively new there, gaining a foothold only with the introduction of Bitcoin and the blockchain. In the Bitcoin literature, as in the central bank conspiracy writings, we read that the Fed is a private bank that hides its real purpose; that it steals money from some private citizens and put it in the hands of the "elites" that control the Fed; that the Fed itself is covertly run by a shadowy group of elites, often made up of Jews and members of English banking families such as the Rothschilds; and so on.

Bitcoin literature also advances the more subtle extremist argument that inflation and deflation are caused by monetary policy rather than by more conventional aspects of economies like consumer prices, commodity and asset prices, productivity and other aspects of labor, and so on. It is a cardinal feature of right-wing financial thought to promote idea that inflation and deflation are the *result* of central bank actions, rather than the far more mainstream view that banks take action to manage inflation or deflation *in response to* external economic pressures. This view is repeated with remarkable persistence and with a remarkable lack of critical examination in a significant portion of discussions about Bitcoin, regardless of their overt politics.

A third pillar of extremist thought we regularly find in Bitcoin circles is less specific to Bitcoin but more endemic in the digital world among cypherpunks, crypto-anarchists, and other advocates of nebulous digital causes like "internet freedom." This is the presumption that computer-based expertise trumps that of all other forms of expertise, sometimes because everything in the world is ultimately reducible to computational processes (a view sometimes known as *computationalism*; see Golumbia 2009). This computer-centric point of view is extremely common throughout digital culture, and it is especially notable in Bitcoin discussions. The implication is that this lack of technical expertise disqualifies the critic from speaking on the topic at all. Of course, no such parallel expertise is granted to fields like economics and finance, despite their own highly technical nature. This selective evaluation of individuals based on a self-nominated set of meaningful and not-meaningful criteria fits uncomfortably well with the tendencies toward *producerism*, *anti-elitism*, and *anti-intellectualism* that critics like Berlet (e.g., 2009, 26) see as endemic in contemporary right-wing movements. Keywords like "elite," "establishment," and "academic," at least at times, signal this rejection of all those forms of non-computational expertise.

A fourth and final pillar of extremist thought is also found both inside and outside Bitcoin discourse, but appears there with particular force: the idea that government itself is inherently evil, distinct in kind from other forms of power but *not* in terms of its responsibility to the democratic polity. Of course this view flows somewhat directly from the anarcho-capitalist thought of Rothbard and the antigovernment neoliberal doctrines of Reagan, Thatcher, and their supporters, the Koch brothers, the Cato and Heritage Foundations, and many more. It also flows directly from the views of crypto-anarchists and cypherpunks, and to only a slightly lesser extent from the general cyberlibertarian predisposition against internet regulation, and the way that many "privacy advocates" focus so much of their energy on what governments are apparently doing and so little on what corporations are provably doing. At the limit, these perspectives suggest not simply that current governments are corrupt or misguided, but that the project of governance itself is an idea whose time has passed, one to be superseded by markets and market-like mechanisms that offer no resistance at all to concentrations of power, and no formal means beyond market forces to hold those who abuse power accountable to the rest of us. Ironically, in so many ways, and yet befitting the actual political work they do in the world, by painting the world today as if it were an ungoverned "tyranny," conspiratorial belief systems help to pave the way for just such tyrannies to emerge.

Not all conspiracy theories are the same, despite the use of that term to disqualify many disparate strands of thought that may at times present themselves as alternatives to orthodox or dominant political views (for recent scholarly treatments of the range of "conspiracy theories" and the various meanings of the term see Birchall 2006; Bratich 2008; see also Mulloy 2005, which offers a solid account of the uses of conspiracy theory by right-wing extremist groups in the United States). Views that appear to be conspiratorial at one time may become established or even proven history at others; conversely, established history can turn out at later moments to have been fabricated. It is not the case that merely labeling an idea "conspiracy theory" means it is necessarily untrue. But the conspiracy theories associated with Bitcoin are among the most deeply entrenched, pervasive, politically charged, yet disproven of all the ongoing lines of political discourse in the United States and Europe. Whatever minor kernel of truth they contain (roughly, that very rich and politically powerful people exercise far more influence over the rest of us than we would like to believe) is almost entirely obscured by the projection of a shadowy, absolutely powerful, fundamentally evil racial or religious Other who is actually responsible for many major world historical events. These theories percolate almost exclusively on the extreme political right and serve (to some extent ironically) to mobilize and contain the political energies of those who subscribe to them. It is these theories that dominate not just Bitcoin rhetoric but also the actual functioning of Bitcoin as software and currency: we might say that Bitcoin activates or executes right-wing extremism, putting into practice what had until recently been theory.

There is much more about Bitcoin, its culture, and even its politics than can be accommodated in a short survey of its profound engagement with right-wing thought and practice. Here, my exclusive goal is to trace out this specific line of thought, both because of its urgency and because it has often been misunderstood by some in the media and is continually misrepresented by Bitcoin propagandists. The point is much less that Bitcoin is attractive to those on the right wing, than it is that Bitcoin and the blockchain themselves depend on right-wing assumptions, and help to spread those assumptions as if they could be separated from the context in which they were generated. Absent an awareness of that context, Bitcoin serves, like much right-wing rhetoric, to spread and firmly root a politics part of whose method is to obscure its material and social functions.

3. An Overview of Bitcoin

MOST PEOPLE FIRST ENCOUNTER BITCOIN as a digital currency (this is shorthand; whether it is a "true" currency is a matter for debate). While Bitcoin is entirely a digital "object," this does not make it much different from other forms of currency that today exist entirely or almost entirely in digital form, even including standard world currencies. One can buy, sell, trade into and out of, and exchange it for other forms of currency, just as one would trade for any other currency. There are exchanges where individuals can buy bitcoins for U.S. dollars, euros, and yen. Like all currencies, there are exchange rates at which these transactions will be processed, and these rates change constantly. When we talk about the "price" of Bitcoin, it is usually relative to one of these world currencies.

Like other forms of digital currency, including ordinary dollars, users can store Bitcoin in an account with something like a "bank," although in Bitcoin's case this is typically an exchange specifically created for this purpose, rather than a more typical bank. Many of these exchanges, such as the now-shuttered Mt. Gox (Rizzo 2014b), have been targets for scams and theft, due in part both to Bitcoin's antigovernment reputation and its hostility to regulation. Unlike other forms of digital currency, users can also run a small piece of software called a "Bitcoin wallet" on their own computers and store their bitcoins there rather than in online accounts.

Bitcoins can be transferred by using one of the many exchanges set up for that purpose, or they can be sent directly to another user's wallet by using an address provided by the wallet holder. That address, like all Bitcoin data, is encrypted: it's a string of letters, numbers, and symbols that mean nothing to anyone without the proper decrypting software and keys: an example would be a string like 1JArS6jzE3AJ9sZ3aFij1BmTcpFGgN86hA. The address is technically the encrypted version of a cryptographic "public key." The address cannot be decoded without the user's "private key." All transactions on the Bitcoin network are public and available to all users of the full Bitcoin software; but since the addresses are encrypted, nothing more about the identity of the wallet holder is necessarily available. Bitcoin is therefore considered *pseudonymous* (Beigel 2015): it is not fully anonymous, since every transaction is recorded, but determining the true identities of those involved in the transactions requires more information than is directly available in the network. The possibility of identifying those true identities and the potential methods for obscuring them altogether are live topics of discussion in the cryptocurrency community (see, e.g., Meiklejohn and Orlandi 2015).

The Bitcoin software does not exist in a single physical location, or in one virtual "cloud" location: it is not hosted by a company like Level 3 or, for that matter, Amazon or Google. Instances of the Bitcoin software run on thousands or tens of thousands of computers all over the world. It depends for its continued life not on any one of those computers, but on the many machines that make up the network. Further, many of those computers—all of the ones running the complete Bitcoin program—host copies of the complete record of *all* Bitcoin transactions, though it is not necessary to host the records to use Bitcoin. That set of records is called the *ledger,* and is conceptually equivalent to the transaction records of other financial entities, such as a bank or brokerage account. These qualities of the Bitcoin software are what lead advocates to describe it as "decentralized" and/or "distributed": there is no single central authority who publishes and maintains the software, so it is "decentralized"; and the software itself sits all over many separate machines on the network, so it is "distributed." A Bitcoin *wallet* is a relatively small piece of software that allows users to keep bitcoins on their own computers without needing to host the full Bitcoin ledger.

The ledger is the first widespread implementation of a software model called a *blockchain.* The techniques involved in building the blockchain work to ensure that transactions are unique and authentic: "The block chain is a shared public ledger on which the entire Bitcoin network relies. All confirmed transactions are included in the block chain. This way, Bitcoin wallets can calculate their spendable balance and new transactions can be verified to be spending bitcoins that are actually owned by the spender. The integrity and the chronological order of the blockchain are enforced with cryptography" ("How Does Bitcoin Work?"). Computers that participate in the verification process are rewarded with fractional amounts of Bitcoin. This is the exclusive means by which Bitcoin is created; the process is known as *mining,* in a deliberate reference to gold. The blockchain is large and processing it requires significant computing power; in fact, because it is a record of *all* Bitcoin transactions ever, any computer participating in Bitcoin mining must today have substantial networking and processing capabilities. While in its early days Bitcoin could be mined by relatively fast home computers, today most mining is done by pools of dedicated high-power systems, due to the increasing difficulty in generating a "hash" designed into the blockchain model. This fact alone has raised significant questions about Bitcoin's claim to "democratize" or "decentralize" currency operations, in part because the system is exposed to the "51 percent problem": if one entity controls more than 51 percent of the mining operations at any one time (something which was at one point unthinkable, but which now has happened at least once), it could, at least theoretically, "change the rules of Bitcoin at any time" (Felten 2014; also see Otar 2015). The amount of power consumed by blockchain operations is large enough that it has suggested to some that Bitcoin itself is "unsustainable" (Malmo 2015). The use of cryptographic techniques is what gives Bitcoin and other technologies like it the descriptive term *cryptocurrency*.

The Bitcoin program is currently "capped," permitting only twenty-one million coins to be "mined." It is limited in this way because its developers believe that the total number of coins in circulation has an impact on the value of the currency. This is an economic rather than a computer science argument, and it is one with which few economists agree. To some extent it derives from Austrian economics and from the monetarist view of inflation propounded by Milton Friedman and others, but it flies in the face of easily observed facts. Bitcoin's price decline from upward of US$1,000 in late 2013 to US$200 in mid-2015 represents something like 500 percent inflation in eighteen months, in the strictest economic terms, despite the supply of Bitcoin increasing only by about 10 percent over that time period ("Controlled Supply"). In other words, and very literally, a product I could buy for 1 BTC in late 2013 would have cost me 5 BTC in mid-2015. One could scarcely ask for a more textbook example of not just inflation but hyperinflation: the fast and brutal destruction of value for those who hold the instrument. There is nothing mysterious about this: gold itself (like all other commodities, whether limited in supply or not) routinely inflates and deflates, without regard to the total amount of the metal available. Yet Bitcoin advocates continue to advertise the cryptocurrency as if it is immune from inflation, discounting the hard evidence before their own eyes. Quite a few apparently responsible pieces (e.g. Vigna and Casey 2015) have made claims like this at the same time that Bitcoin has been experiencing not just inflation but hyperinflation of exactly the sort Federal Reserve "critics" claim to fear most.

The Bitcoin software has a distinct origin point, in a 2008 paper titled "Bitcoin: A Peer-to-Peer Electronic Cash System," by a pseudonymous author who called himself "Satoshi Nakamoto." Yet we need to reach back deeper into history to grasp Bitcoin's complete political and intellectual contexts. Most of those involved in the development and early adoption of Bitcoin were and are part of several intersecting communities who have long put a huge amount of faith into very specific technological–political orientations toward the world, ones grounded in overtly right-wing thought, typically coupled with myopic technological utopianism. These include movements like Extropians, cypherpunks, crypto-anarchists, political libertarians with an interest in technology, transhumanists, Singularitarians, and a wide swath of self-described hackers and open source software developers. Sometimes the politics of these individuals and the groups in which they travel are inchoate, but often enough they are explicit (see Carrico 2009, 2013a, 2013b for detailed discussions of these various movements, focusing in particular on their politics). Yet even Nakamoto himself, in one of the first announcements that the Bitcoin system was actually running, rested his justification for the creation of the system on the extremist story about inflation and central banks: "The root problem with conventional currency is all the trust that's required to make it work. The central bank must be trusted not to debase the currency, but the history of fiat currencies is full of breaches of that trust. Banks must be trusted to hold our money and transfer it electronically, but they lend it out in waves of credit bubbles with barely a fraction in reserve" (Nakamoto 2009). Ironically, Nakamoto seems not to have realized that his belief that Bitcoin would be immune to "debasement" was based on a flawed monetarist definition of inflation, or that Bitcoin itself could fuel credit bubbles and fractional reserve banking.

Journalist Nathaniel Popper, in the most thorough history to date of Bitcoin and its connection to these groups (Popper 2015), draws attention to the role of so-called crypto-anarchists and cypherpunks in what would eventually become Bitcoin (for analyses of the direct connections among Bitcoin, cypherpunks, and crypto-anarchists see Boase 2013; DuPont 2014; for this story from the perspective of Bitcoin promoters see Lopp 2016; Redman 2015). Among the clearest targets of these movements (see both the "Cypherpunk's Manifesto," Hughes 1993; and the closely related "Crypto-Anarchist Manifesto," May 1992) has always specifically been governmental *oversight* of financial (and other) transactions. No effort is made to distinguish between legitimate and illegitimate use of governmental power: rather, *all* governmental power is inherently taken to be illegitimate. Further, despite occasional rhetorical nods toward corporate abuses, just as in Murray Rothbard's work, strictly speaking no mechanisms whatsoever are posited that actually might constrain corporate power. Combined with either an explicit commitment toward, or at best an extreme naïveté about, the operation of concentrated capital, this political theory works to deprive the people of their only proven mechanism for that constraint. This is why as august an antigovernment thinker as Noam Chomsky (2015) can have declared that libertarian theories, despite surface appearances, promote "corporate tyranny, meaning tyranny by unaccountable private concentrations of power, the worst kind of tyranny you can imagine."

Even at their brief length, both May's and Hughes's manifestoes nod toward "markets" and "open societies," both of them keywords for the right in the United States since Hayek (on the rightist foundations of the concept of "open society," particularly as it relies on the thought of Mont Pelerin member Karl Popper, see Tkacz 2012). Both May and Hughes, like most rightist populists in the United States, presume that politics is organized exclusively around the sovereign individual who expresses himself through the power he accumulates; both craft artificial and unjustified distinctions between good people who are like myself and deserve a kind of absolute protection *from* the law, while (often simultaneously) invoking rhetoric of natural law and human or civil rights. They shift responsibility for lawbreaking and antisocial behavior to some nebulous but determinate "others" whose bad acts are to be steered around by technical means (Payne 2013 does a particularly good job of relating this point of view to Bitcoin; also see Scott 2014). They reject the fundamental equality of human beings based on citizenship or respect, and instead assert the rights of specially appointed (and self-appointed) actors, themselves, to fundamentally alter the terms of governance, without so much as the knowledge, let alone the assent, of the governed—in short, they subscribe to an extreme version of "might makes right," and the only equality they are interested in is the ability of each person to empower himself fully against the claims of others. May (1992) writes, "The State will of course try to slow or halt the spread of this technology, citing national security concerns, use of the technology by drug dealers and tax evaders, and fears of societal disintegration. Many of these concerns will be valid; crypto anarchy will allow national secrets to be traded freely and will allow illicit and stolen materials to be traded." Despite the validity of its concerns (which, it should be noted, more recent cypherpunk activists have been even less willing to grant than was May), the state's efforts "will not halt the spread of crypto anarchy." To the degree that Bitcoin realizes the dreams of May and Hughes and the other cypherpunks, it is a dream of using software to dismantle the very project of representative governance, at the bidding of nobody but technologists and in particular technologists who loathe the political apparatus others have developed. That many of these same crypto-anarchist and cypherpunk technologists—to say nothing of the Bitcoin entrepreneurs who work closely with major Silicon Valley venture capitalists—today sit at or near the heads of the world's major corporations tells us everything we need to know about their attitude toward concentrated corporate power (May himself worked at Intel for more than a decade).

One of the most prominent canards used to defend Bitcoin against allegations of its profoundly right-wing nature is to suggest that Bitcoin is advocated by some who see themselves as on the political left, and that only a subset of those deeply involved in the promotion of Bitcoin describe themselves as libertarian. One of the "myths" supposedly debunked on the Bitcoin wiki is given as "the Bitcoin community consists of anarchist / conspiracy theorist / gold standard 'weenies,'" to which the response offered is the following: "The members of the community vary in their ideological stances. While it may have been started by ideological enthusiasts, Bitcoin now speaks to a large number of regular pragmatic folk, who

33

simply see its potential for reducing the costs and friction of global e-commerce" ("Myths"). Defenses like this take the notion of "political affiliation" too literally, as overtly declared party allegiance.[1] They are part of what fuel the "magical thinking" (Payne 2013) according to which Bitcoin can be advertised as "apolitical" and at the same time profoundly political (see Kostakis and Giotitsas 2014; Varoufakis 2013). Yet what is critical about Bitcoin discourse, like other parts of cyberlibertarian discourse, is less the overtly political alliances of those who engage with it than the politics that is entailed by their practice. In Bitcoin promotion, these arise especially with regard to corporate and governmental power (Bitcoin evangelists routinely promote the former, so long as it is favorable toward Bitcoin, and disparage the latter) and the dissemination of views about the nature of money and governmental oversight of money. It is not only those who see themselves as libertarians who, through the adoption of Bitcoin and the political communities around it, routinely distribute political and economic views that are grounded in conspiratorial, far-right accounts of the Federal Reserve and the nature of representative government. Whatever its success as a currency, Bitcoin has proved incredibly useful for spreading these views, to some extent shorn of the marks of their political origins, but no less useful for the powerful corporate interests who benefit from other aspects of rightist discourse.

1. A similar and related problem is found in a widely cited study that purports to determine that "political motives" do not drive Bitcoin use by examining Google Trends data for evidence of libertarians using the cryptocurrency. The study examines Google searches that combine Bitcoin-related terms with the phrase "free market" (Wilson and Yelowitz 2014, 4), without providing any control data to demonstrate that searches for the term "free market" tell us anything at all about political affiliation or political–economic practice.

Widespread interest in Bitcoin first emerged from its utility as a means to bypass the "WikiLeaks blockade." As put in 2012 by Jon Matonis, founding board member and executive director of the Bitcoin Foundation until he resigned in October 2014 (Casey 2014) and one of Bitcoin's most vocal advocates:

> Following a massive release of secret U.S. diplomatic cables in November 2010, donations to WikiLeaks were blocked by Bank of America, VISA, MasterCard, PayPal, and Western Union on December 7th, 2010. Although private companies certainly have a right to select which transactions to process or not, the political environment produced less than a fair and objective decision. It was coordinated pressure exerted in a politicized climate by the U.S. government and it won't be the last time that we see this type of pressure.
>
> Fortunately, there is way around this and other financial blockades with a global payment method immune to political pressure and monetary censorship. (Matonis 2012b)

Bitcoin made it possible for individuals to donate to WikiLeaks despite it being a violation of U.S. law to do so. In Matonis's view, corporations participating with U.S. government laws is illegitimate and amounts to "censorship" and "political pressure": there is simply no consideration of the idea that it might be appropriate for financial providers to cooperate with the government against efforts that directly and purposely contravene perfectly valid law (regardless of whether one agrees with that law). Despite the fact that Bitcoin appears here to be operating against corporate power, what Matonis paints is a picture—one confirmed by the rhetoric surrounding newer proposals like blockchain-based corporations (see chapter 6)—of corporate and financial power operating without oversight and outside the constraints of governmental power. It's clear that Matonis and others would very much have liked Visa,

MasterCard, and other businesses to have refused to cooperate with the requests made by the governments under whose laws they exist at all.

In the contexts of finance and money, the word "regulation" has two distinct meanings that can easily be conflated. The first is *central bank modulation of the value of the dollar*: this is what Bitcoin enthusiasts and right-wing conspiracy theorists refer to when they talk about the Federal Reserve "devaluing" U.S. currency by "printing more money." The second meaning, less frequently invoked but critical when it is mentioned, relates to the kinds of statutory oversight practiced by the U.S. Securities and Exchange Commission (SEC), with regard to financial markets, and to U.S. agencies like the Food and Drug Administration, the Environmental Protection Agency, the Occupational Safety and Health Administration, and the Equal Employment Opportunity Commission.

These agencies, technically members of the executive branch, have been the targets of right-wing ire, especially since they expanded in scope and power during the New Deal. The "Lochner era" of Supreme Court jurisprudence, typically said to extend from about 1897 through to 1937, and overlapping to some extent with the "robber baron era," marked a period of severe constraint on the powers of the federal government to regulate business practices, under a doctrine known as "substantive due process" (see Gillman 1995 for a general overview). It is no accident that the birth of modern U.S. right-wing extremism coincides with the demise of Lochner, as the forms of regulatory oversight that were once again made legitimate then placed significant constraints on corporate power, and the animus toward this form of oversight, generated by corporate titans and those whose wealth depends on corporations, continues in a fairly unbroken line from the late 1930s through to the present day (see Zuesse 2015 for a particularly pointed assessment of this history). Despite the frequent use of populist rhetoric by these movements, they have never been less than direct bids for corporate sovereignty over against democratic powers that seek, however imperfectly, to constrain what corporations do. The arguments against regulation have very little to recommend them outside the consolidation of corporate power, other than a certain reasonable concern about the amount of bureaucracy that might be involved in certain everyday endeavors; the arguments in favor have any number of serious and meaningful justifications, many of them directly implicated in the securing of life, liberty, and the pursuit of happiness.

When Bitcoin enthusiasts extol the currency's existence beyond "regulation by nation-states," they frequently blur the lines between these two very different forms of regulation, which really are unconnected except at the most abstract level. After all, the Federal Reserve, as right-wing extremists never tire of pointing out, is not part of the government; OSHA, the EPA, the SEC, and the other agencies all are. The Fed has no direct enforcement power, whereas regulatory agencies typically do. The Fed's charge is twofold: to keep the unemployment rate relatively low, and to try to assure a constant, relatively modest rate of inflation. These are both modulatory effects: it is not a criminal or even civil violation for the inflation rate to get too high. Regulatory agencies, on the other hand, are concerned with implementing federal laws, most of which have been passed specifically to protect the health, safety, and/or welfare of U.S. citizens. They have a variety of powers to charge or to recommend charges of a criminal or civil nature against third parties, especially corporations, when those laws are violated. Both kinds of regulation are relevant to the distribution and use of money like the U.S. dollar, in different ways. Bitcoin is obviously built to escape the kind of regulation the Federal Reserve exerts over U.S. interest rates and the money supply (which I'll refer to as "money supply regulation" in what follows), yet this is frequently taken to mean that it somehow inherently escapes the second kind of regulation (which I'll call "legal regulation") despite there being very little reason to think that might be true.

Some of the issues in legal regulation that Bitcoin enthusiasts routinely say their currency addresses are ones with significant justification in law enforcement—thus, statutes making money laundering illegal, forcing banks to report transactions over US$10,000, having limits on international transfers, and so on. Typically, Bitcoin defenders respond to criticisms of the cryptocurrency based on such deficiencies by pointing out that cash transactions can face at least some of the same complications (e.g., Patron 2015, 33–34; Brito and Castillo 2013, 37). While nominally correct, such after-the-fact justifications cannot bear the weight placed on them. That one instrument has a flaw does not imply that we must accept new instruments with the same flaw. Further, a huge part of its appeal is that Bitcoin enables instantaneous, worldwide, digital transfers of wealth, something that advocates are quick to point out paper money and physical commodities cannot do. It is question begging to say that we must accept Bitcoin for having certain similarities to existing media of exchange: if it were the case that Bitcoin is just the same as physical cash, we would not be having a discussion about Bitcoin. Bitcoin is not the same as physical cash. So we cannot dismiss criticisms of it by emphasizing their similarities, unless we are also prepared to abandon Bitcoin altogether for physical cash. (This form of question-begging justification is a commonplace in digital culture; see Golumbia 2013a.)

Some of the more interesting moments in Bitcoin discourse occur when advocates of one form or another appear to realize that these forms of regulation are not identical. This has occurred particularly often when one of the many Bitcoin exchanges has defrauded its users. Remarkably, at these moments, some of the most ardent opponents of "government regulation" turn out to regret deeply the absence of exactly those features of government regulation (as well as some of the functions of intermediaries) that they have fought against so relentlessly. See, for example, Bitcoin evangelist Rick Falkvinge (2013a), who argues that although Bitcoin's "unenforceability of governmental rules is a feature, not a bug," manipulations of the Bitcoin market, which he calls "illegal trading activity," are "cheating of some kind, a breaking of the social contract," while noting that there is an "irony" in people using unregulated instruments to engage in just the activities regulation is designed to prohibit. The irony is not in that usage; it is in the typically right-wing insistence that eliminating regulations will somehow eliminate the behavior that the regulations exist specifically to prevent.

4. Central Banking Conspiracy Theories

FEDERAL RESERVE CONSPIRACY THEORIES are the most prominent elements of far-right propaganda found in Bitcoin commentary. This is not to suggest a direct genealogical connection between, for example, Mullins's writings and Bitcoin evangelism, much less control of Bitcoin discourse by right-wing propagandists like the Koch brothers or the think tanks they fund, but it is important to understand that this is not the exclusive or even primary way that ideologies work. Rather, these ideas catch on where they serve a need or fill a desire and where there is an opening for them (both Berlet and Lyons 2000; and Diamond 1995 provide excellent analyses of the reasons for the success of right-wing ideas in the United States). Bitcoin software has helped to create that opening, and the needs its ideology serves are the same ones served by Jones, Makow, Icke, and others. While there may in fact be direct connections between some of the more prominent conspiracy theorists and Bitcoin propaganda (one that is exacerbated by the promotion of Bitcoin in right-wing conspiracy forums), it is more likely that, and no less politically salient if, these tropes simply found a ready home in certain aspects of Bitcoin's social and technical characteristics.

It is nevertheless remarkable how closely Bitcoin rhetoric replicates specific elements of right-wing Federal Reserve conspiracism. Late in 2013, as the price in U.S. dollars of Bitcoin began to surge, outgoing U.S. Federal Reserve chair Ben Bernanke made a statement before the U.S. Senate Committee on Homeland Security and Governmental Affairs in part about Bitcoin and similar technologies, in which he explained that the Fed "does not have authority to directly supervise or regulate these innovations or the entities that provide them to the market." Among the sixty-two comments made to just one brief story (Farivar 2013) reporting these hearings on the relatively levelheaded technology site Ars Technica, we find the following:

The argument that fiat allows a country to avoid debasement is spurious at best given that monetary printing beyond demand either to spur economic growth, or collect seigniorage, is just like debasement in the end result's decreasing purchasing power of nominal values. (user k2000k)[1]

The Fed isn't a part of the government. It's a privately owned bank, the shareholders, of which, are kept secret. They have exactly zero authority on monetary policy. They impose their control over the money supply by adjusting the interest rate on loans they give to other banks. (user greevar)

We entrust Congress with the power to declare war, regulate trade, raise an army with really cool weapons to blow things up, decide what we can be imprisoned or put to death for, decide what types of foods we can eat, etc. . . . but we can't trust them with printing money. If you believe that last part then you should also be against any form of tax which puts our money in their hands. (user soulsabr)

1. All reader comments have been lightly standardized for spelling and punctuation.

Executive Order 6102 was passed to steal gold from the citizens of America [and put it] into Ft. Knox so that they could have leverage to inflate currency at will. It ensures that no child will have an inheritance that cannot be devalued over time. Self-sufficiency is the enemy of control; economic slavery in the name of profit and prosperity for the few. (user Vapur9)

Since slavery was outlawed, they needed a new way to get people to work for their "American Dream." Independent, self-sufficient, and prosperous citizens don't meet that criteria; so, they passed a new method by abusing the law-making process. Unfortunately, the aims of prosperity are leading us to societal decay at an even faster pace because we all see the sky falling. (user Vapur9)

Each of these comments uses language and ideas from right-wing extremism without identifying itself as such. An unsuspecting reader—and for that matter an unsuspecting commentator—might believe these sentiments to be unobjectionable statements of fact, thus priming themselves to accept several lines of conspiratorial belief while having never opened a book by Eustace Mullins or a JBS pamphlet.

This pattern is the rule rather than the exception. It is rare to find any story on Bitcoin regardless of venue—from mainstream publications to the far reaches of the Bitcoin-centric universe—that does not elicit significant and sustained commentary in which bedrock precepts of right-wing conspiracism are presented as if they are obvious and uncontestable statements of fact. Thus, on the thoughtfully critical economics blog Naked Capitalism, largely populated by well-informed readers, regarding a post titled "Everything I Was Afraid to Ask about Bitcoin but Did" (Murray 2013), in which the author notes that promotion of the currency depends on a certain "circularity of arguments about trust," one commentator responds:

The bitcoin purpose, and its primary attraction is it can't be manipulated, devalued, by central banks the way fiat can. As for volatility, all I can say is "bitcoin cost averaging" :)

It always seems to end up higher than it was a few weeks ago. The same can't be said for fiat. Why would I want to pay some banker fee to get into a security when my currency can go up in value without any fees at all? (user R Foreman)

Here "central bank manipulation" is posited as the destruction of value, while Bitcoin's utility as an investment—as I discuss below, nothing more or less than the selfsame "destruction of value"—is touted as a virtue. When another commentator, "DakatobornKansan," writes that "what doomed communism, and will likely undermine Bitcoin, is the delusional hope that a protocol, a procedure, a network, an algorithm can neutralize the ugly selfish traits of human beings," user "Robert Dudek" quotes the comment and writes, "'This could just as easily be applied to Central Banking.'"

Of course, when we look to sites already aligned with the right, even if they usually avoid conspiracy theory, engagement with Bitcoin results in a veritable deluge of extremist sentiment. Paul Krugman's 2013 article "Bitcoin Is Evil" produced a wealth of conspiratorial commentary on the *New York Times* site where it was originally published, and even more outraged commentary in social media and on blogs. A typical response was found on the rightist economics blog Against Crony Capitalism, whose editor Nick Sorrentino wrote a piece titled "Paul Krugman Is Scared: He Says 'Bitcoin Is Evil': Undermines Central Banks" (2013). Others immediately leapt to discredit Krugman's authority altogether (see Gongloff 2013; Yarow 2013). Comments to the piece itself include user "Michael Werner" noting that *"The Creature from Jekyll Island* gives a great history of the Fed and the damage it's done over the years"; user "Oh Be Newman" writing that "undermining central banks is EXACTLY what we need!!!!!"; user "Glen Pfeiffer" stating that "the Fed is evil incarnate"; user "Scott B Handley" stating that "based on the 'central' bank's records—I guess evil is a prerequisite"; and user "Anthony Morales" stating that "it's all a scam: money should be nationalized, period. Every government should print and control its currency not no egotistical spoiled tyrants like the Rothschilds Morgans and the rest of the banking cartel they're the reasons behind war poverty and hunger I'm sorry but if I could I would persecute all of them just like they did to innocent people throughout history." Nearly all of the approximately one hundred comments to the story are of this tone and content, other than those that viciously target Krugman himself (e.g., user "Uwe Koch," who calls Krugman a "commie cocksucker"). Unsurprisingly, Sorrentino's post was enthusiastically reprinted by the Infowars website of major right-wing conspiracist Alex Jones.

One of the sites of most significant overlap between Bitcoin discourse and far-right political extremism can be seen with particular clarity in the use of the right-wing keywords "tyranny" and "liberty." The most florid claim of Bitcoin advocates is that Bitcoin poses "an existential threat to the nation-state," because nation-states supposedly live in fear that their hold on monetary policy via central banks like the Federal Reserve is threatened by the existence of alternatives to money (e.g., Soltas 2013). Jon Matonis wrote during Bitcoin's first wave of wide publicity in 2012 that "Bitcoin prevents monetary tyranny" and that "just as the Second Amendment in the United States, at its core, remains the final right of a free people to prevent their ultimate political repression, a powerful instrument is needed to prevent a corresponding repression—State monetary supremacy" (Matonis 2012a).

Much of the literature promoting it—including books issued by reputable presses and self-published by enthusiasts, and articles from blog posts to pieces in leading publications like the *New York Times*, the *Wall Street Journal*, and *Forbes*—appears to be about nothing more or less than Bitcoin, the technology that underlies it and its practical uses in the world. Yet again and again, themes, ideas, keywords, and arguments from right-wing extremist thought appear, often stated as uncontroversial fact. Thus, leading venture capitalist and Netscape Navigator creator Marc Andreessen, in a *New York Times* piece that is on the whole balanced and sober, writes that Bitcoin data is relayed "through a distributed network of trust that does not require or rely upon a central intermediary like a bank or broker" (Andreessen 2014), taking for granted that this "requirement" or "reliance" is somehow something one would obviously want to avoid—but this is an idea, at least until recently, we find only in right-wing circles. Then Andreessen writes that "political idealists project visions of liberation and revolution onto it; establishment elites heap contempt and scorn on it." But very few outside the right would see the people Andreessen is referring to as "idealists" ("ideologues" might be a more reasonable description), and the language of "establishment elites" is, especially given the context, too close an echo of JBS propaganda not to seem shocking when it occurs without comment in a major U.S. newspaper.

If Andreessen's language includes unfortunate and possibly even unconscious reference to extremist ideas, the comments on his piece display no such consideration. User "Small Biz Owner" relates Bitcoin directly to Milton Friedman, and writes that "to be able to transfer money anywhere in the world instantly and without scrutiny from the IRS and the gilded Wall Street banks would be a revolution in the world's monetary system," displaying the typical right-wing disdain for taxation and desire to be free of law and regulation. User "Dombah" celebrates the idea that we might be able to validate a transaction ledger "without the need of a central governing authority." And user "Eric" writes:

> Cashing out [from Bitcoin] into USD would only devalue the transactions. The goal is to eliminate cash money in order to eliminate inflation based off printing Monopoly money printed by Governments. It seems far-fetched, but finding a supplier in a Country that I can buy goods for resell that accepted Bitcoin would allow me to earn 5% more right away. And selling to someone who would pay with Bitcoin would just increase the value of the goods sold. I will be able to buy for less and sell for less, others will have to pay more and sell for a higher price thus, feeding the Government its entitled fixed percentage of your business that they control by inflating the currency they provide. STOP letting the Government be the middlemen, they don't have our best interests at hand.

This last comment, of a kind that is very typical in Bitcoin discussions regardless of venue, rehearses virtually the whole of conspiracist economics and political theory, especially the allegation that the "government" exists to deprive individuals of "value," that taxes ("its entitled fixed percentage of your business") are to be avoided entirely if possible, and that central banks "print" money and this causes value-destructive inflation about which we should all be worried.

Conspiratorial accounts of inflation and deflation are often key elements of "mainstream" Bitcoin presentations. Self-described "serial entrepreneur" and "Bitcoin entrepreneur" Andreas M. Antonopoulos was chosen by O'Reilly Media, perhaps the leading publisher of books about digital technology, to write its first entry into the Bitcoin market, *Mastering Bitcoin* (2014). As one would expect, the book includes a fairly detailed and clearly written account of Bitcoin technology, the use of Bitcoin as a currency, and so on. But in what should be surprising for a book ostensibly about technology, it also includes several substantial economic discussions in which extremist views are proffered, without attribution, as if they are simply common-sense analyses of relatively uncontroversial subjects. Antonopoulos offers matter-of-fact accounts of Bitcoin technology that incorporate conspiratorial theories about the Federal Reserve: "bitcoin mining decentralizes the currency-issuance and clearing functions of a central bank and replaces the need for any central bank with this global competition [to mine for bitcoins]" (2); "mining creates new bitcoins in each block, almost like a central bank printing new money" (26).

Among the most remarkable passages in this technical book is one in which Antonopoulos rewrites the economics of deflation in a way that serves the interests of Bitcoin promoters like himself, but at the same time dismisses out of hand almost all non-conspiratorial work on the topic. He does this not by mounting a sustained and detailed argument against the various economic accounts of deflation, but simply by providing his own ad-hoc argument that takes as a given a conspiratorial account of deflation (and its inverse, inflation). Antonopoulos does not refer to any economist, private or academic, when he states that "many economists argue that a deflationary economy is a disaster that should be avoided at all costs. That is because in a period of rapid deflation, people tend to hoard money instead of spending it, hoping that prices will fall" (176), failing to point out that he is being ambiguous about "spending" in passages like this, since it is much less consumer spending than *production* spending that makes deflation so destructive, because producers earn more money by saving than by manufacturing products. Antonopoulos then offers a completely ad-hoc account of economic cycles: "The hoarding instinct caused by a deflationary currency can be overcome by discounting from vendors, until the discount overcomes the hoarding instinct of the buyer. Because the seller is also motivated to hoard, the discount becomes the equilibrium price at which the two hoarding instincts are matched. With discounts of 30% on the Bitcoin price, most Bitcoin retailers are not experiencing difficulty overcoming the hoarding instinct and generating revenue. It remains to be seen whether the deflationary aspect of the currency is really a problem when it is not driven by rapid economic retraction" (176). This argument builds on the conspiratorial account of deflation (and inflation) to admit and then abruptly dismiss well-established economic principles, to Bitcoin's advantage. "Discounting from vendors," especially when seen from the perspective of producers rather than of retailers, is nothing more or less than accepting substantial losses as a simple price of doing business, which may be reasonable as an intermittent practice or for ideological reasons, but is clearly in direct violation of the very market principles that Bitcoin is supposed to realize.

Even when Bitcoin promoters claim to reject right-wing politics, they frequently take them on board anyway, further obscuring the political valence of their analyses. In a typically dismissive and sweeping piece on Falkvinge.net devoted to the question of whether "blockchain technology [can] help build a foundation for real democracy," where "real democracy" is contrasted to representative democracy and Bitcoin is posited "as the new First Amendment app," Nozomi Hayase (2015) discusses the "tyranny of central banks" and writes, "In tracing the history of money creation in the United States, attorney and author Ellen Brown [2008] revealed that the real trigger for the Revolutionary War was King George's ban on the printing of local money in the American colonies. She described how after independence was won, the King's economic subservience was not achieved by force but instead by the British bankers persuading the American people to take their paper money." She goes on: "The founding fathers' failure to define exactly what money was along with the lack of healthy parameters around its creation and control left a loophole within this system of representation for the shadowy forces to penetrate and later subvert the Constitution and further betray the ideals in the Declaration. The amorphous centralized creation of money has become a single point of failure that makes the entire system vulnerable to counter-party risk. This was seen especially in the Wall Street hijack of the monetary system with the passing of the Federal Reserve Act in 1913." This is nearly word-forword the Federal Reserve conspiracy theory of Mullins, Griffin, and Larson, filtered through Brown, whose undocumented revisionist history of the United States differs very little from and draws extensively on those of more explicitly right-wing authors. One notes in particular the typical conspiratorial assertion that "shadowy forces . . . penetrate and later subvert the Constitution." Remarks like this are not the exception in Bitcoin discourse; they are the rule.

5. Software as Political Program

WHILE WE HAVE SO FAR DISCUSSED it as *currency*, its advocates frequently promote Bitcoin as a new form of *money* (see, e.g., Emery and Stewart 2015; Smart 2015). Money and currency are not identical. "Money," as we use the word today and as economists define it in standard textbooks, serves three critical functions: *medium of exchange, store of value,* and *unit of account* (see, e.g., Abel, Bernanke, and Croushore 2008, 248–49).[1] *Medium of exchange* means that a token (which need not be physical; a token might be nothing more than an entry in an accounting ledger) can be used to buy or sell products and services; *store of value* means that the tokens can be saved, and (despite a certain level of inherent volatility) can be relied on to maintain their purchasing power. *Unit of account,* sometimes also called *measure of value,* refers to the fact that the market uses the token in determining the value of products, which is to say, their prices. It is worth noting that, in circular reasoning typical of ideological constructions, these textbook definitions

---

1. On Bitcoin's failure to meet the standard criteria for money see Yermack (2014), Davidson (2013), and Gans (2013). Even some responsible libertarian economists demur from the claim that Bitcoin could be money; see, e.g., Shostak (2013).

of money are frequently rejected by Bitcoin advocates, even as they insist that Bitcoin is money. That is, though Bitcoin fails to meet the criteria we have long used to identify money, we are told that we must accept that Bitcoin *is* money (see, e.g., both "Myths"; and Smart 2015 for conspiratorial redefinitions of "money").

Of these three classical functions, it is arguable that Bitcoin serves only as a *medium of exchange*. It is possible to buy and sell products using Bitcoin. Speaking very roughly, "medium of exchange" might well be thought of as the "currency function" of money. As many economists have pointed out, though, virtually *anything* can serve as a medium of exchange, and nonmonetary media of exchange proliferate in our world: from frequent flyer miles to credit card bonus point programs, from grocery store coupons to high-value goods like fine art, precious metals, and gems.[2] None of these alternative currencies poses any threat whatsoever to national sovereignty over money, let alone national sovereignty itself. Yet Bitcoin advocates frequently attempt to redefine money as if the term refers only to medium of exchange.

Whether Bitcoin serves the *unit of account* or *measure of value* function is much less clear. It is rare, though not unheard of, for markets to exist that price their goods only in Bitcoin, and rarer still for those prices to exist in relation to nothing other than Bitcoin: that is to say, even the infamous deep web drug marketplaces like Silk Road and its various offshoots clearly set the Bitcoin prices for their goods according to their value in official world currencies, despite having prices nominally listed in Bitcoin (i.e., those prices rise and fall with changes not just in

2. On Bitcoin's similarity to the wide spectrum of nonmonetary media of exchange, such as "chocolate Hanukkah coins, casino chips, monopoly money, and your frequent flyer miles," see Gans (2013).

Bitcoin's valuation, but in the price of drugs in national curren-cies). Exactly because Bitcoin lacks any relationship to bodies that need the currency to exist in relationship to mechanisms of international exchange, or of state-internal matters like tax-es, Bitcoin on its own floats free of any anchor to ordinary valu-ing processes. If Bitcoin-only economies were to develop, in which labor were priced in raw relation to Bitcoin regardless of Bitcoin's exchange value with world currencies (i.e., labor is priced at 1 BTC an hour regardless of whether 1 BTC is worth US$10 or US$1,000), this situation might change, but this presents the same chicken-and-egg problem we see through-out Bitcoin propaganda: *if* states were to go away and *if* entire economies existed in Bitcoin, *then* it could become money; but it is simultaneously said to be Bitcoin that will *cause* states to wither away and that will produce those economies.

The third function, *store of value,* is Bitcoin's fundamental and most interesting obstacle, and the place where conspir-atorial economic thought becomes most clearly implicated in the structure and usage of the software itself. Part of why Bitcoin is so well-known is precisely *because of* its volatili-ty: it was Bitcoin's remarkable climb to over US$1,000 that brought it to general public attention. Despite the fact that this is seen by many Bitcoin promoters as a "positive" change in value, a change is a change regardless of direction. An in-strument that grows to 400 percent of its original value (from US$200 to US$1,000) in under a year can and will lose 80 percent of its value in a similar time period. A person storing their savings or profits from business in Bitcoin has absolute-ly no reason to expect that that value will be maintained over even a short time frame, and in fact has every reason to ex-pect that it will not.

Bitcoin's status—or lack of status—as store of value is a crucial site at which to observe the currency's ideological functions. One of the most frequent conspiratorial frames for the promotion of Bitcoin is gold itself, or "the gold standard," itself a critical nexus point for conspiratorial financial theory. Bitcoin is routinely promoted as if it constitutes or could constitute a "real" or "sound" store of value the way gold purportedly does, and is often championed in the same right-wing media that sells precious metals as an alternative to the "debased" nation currencies that are said to have lost all their value via inflation. Bitcoin advocates make repeated reference to the superiority of gold-backed money, despite the fact that governments fixed even the price of gold at many moments in history to tame volatility, and in the face of current stories about gold and silver prices being part of the Libor price-fixing scandal.[3] This preference for gold versus what they somewhat inaccurately call the "fiat currency" of nation-states only shows the ideological nature of their assertions, since gold exists right now, is widely traded and can be untraceable, largely resistant to counterfeiting, and yet is widely used (though not as a currency peg) *by the very nation-states and central banks* that Bitcoin advocates say they are in the process of dismantling. Just as revealing are statements like those by self-described "currency trader and economics nerd" Brian Kelly, who in *The Bitcoin Big Bang* inaccurately attributes the threefold nature of money to currency, and despite this, after laying out the case that Bitcoin only serves the medium-of-exchange function, suggests that "we are too tethered to the conventional definition of a currency as a medium

3. For the view that gold-backed money is superior and that Bitcoin is valuable because it is "like gold," see, e.g., Liu (2013). On the historical fixing of gold prices, see "Gold Fix." On the potential implication of gold and silver price fixing in the Libor scandal, see Goodley (2013).

of exchange, a store of value, and a unit of account" (2015, 13). Bitcoin therefore is at once everything that money is, but to the degree it turns out not to be everything that money is, the definition is what's wrong. The problem is that the definition provided by economists is descriptive, not normative: it says that *the money function* as we understand it is only filled by objects that have those three characteristics, not that this is how things *should* be. This kind of semantic play is typical of ideological constructions, but not of serious analysis.

Indeed, the story told so far has if anything tilted the story too much in Bitcoin's favor. For while the textbook account of money includes the three critical functions we have mentioned, the majority of expert economic theory simply defines money as *currency that is issued by a sovereign government*. This theory is known as "Modern Monetary Theory" (MMT) or "neo-chartalism" and has its roots in economics going back at least to John Maynard Keynes, whose views have perpetually been a major target for every sort of attack from right-wing thinkers. According to this view, the difference between *money* and *currency* is that *money is currency issued by the state* and indicates the form of currency in which taxes must be paid. It is precisely the pegging of a given national currency to factors like taxation, national industrial production, and international trade that enables the store of value and unit of account functions of money. That is, nation-state sovereignty and the very idea of *money* are inextricably linked in our world, and so the notion of money that is not issued by a nation-state is essentially a contradiction. Like most right-wing discourses, Bitcoin rhetoric thrives on such paradoxical constructions.[4]

4. Schroeder (2015) closely reads the Uniform Commercial Code to indicate that Bitcoin cannot be classified as money. The U.S. Commodities Futures Trading Commission suggested in late 2014 that

One of the places in which this conundrum is most visible is in the claims of Bitcoin advocates about "fiat money," also an important trope in right-wing extremism. As a general idea, the notion of "fiat currency" has a long history in economics. For example, decades prior to the development of Bitcoin, liberal economist John Kenneth Galbraith (1975, 63) offered the following typology of money:

> Writers on money have regularly distinguished between three types of currency: (1) that which owes its value, as do gold or silver, to an inherent desirability derived from well-established service to pride of possession, prestige of ownership, personal adornment, dinner service or dentistry; (2) that which can readily be exchanged for something of such inherent desirability or which carries the promise, like the early Massachusetts Bay notes, of eventual exchange; and (3) currency which is intrinsically worthless, carries no promise that it will be redeemed in anything useful or desirable and which is sustained, at most, by the fiat of the state that it be accepted.

Note to begin with that Bitcoin does not conform to *any* of these descriptions. At best it is a variation on (3), since what distinguishes (3), "fiat money," from the other two, is that whatever token is being exchanged has no "intrinsic value"—that is, where the token used as currency for that money has demonstrable value in another context. The most typical example of non-fiat currency is gold, because gold has many uses and is still valuable even when not in circulation as currency; paper

---

it would probably classify Bitcoin as a commodity and not a currency, and formally asserted that classification in a legal settlement in September 2015 (Marx 2015). Some closely involved with Bitcoin have suggested that it is an entirely new kind of phenomenon, a "Money-Like Informational Commodity," but base this definition on profoundly tendentious definitions of economic terms; see Swanson (2014).

money, on the other hand, is taken to be fiat because the paper on which it is printed is nearly valueless as paper.

Frequently in Bitcoin discussions, one reads the circular assessment that "fiat" in "fiat money" refers to the "fiat" of the state—that is, an official decree—that turns a currency into money. While there is an element of truth to this, it does not reflect the history and usage of the term "fiat money": since money is inherently a creation of the state, regardless of whether it is based on a token of intrinsic value, even a gold standard would be "fiat currency" according to this definition. One suspects that "fiat by the state" is used in these definitions because the thought of some non-state actor deliberately suggesting that it could flout national law and declare its own currency to be "money" would have been unthinkable until very recently. But there is no way around the fact that Bitcoin advocates have no mechanism *except* fiat by which to declare their currency to be money. The point of the "fiat" label is to distinguish currencies with "intrinsic value" from those without it because these otherwise nearly worthless tokens have been declared to be of value by (someone's) fiat. Further, this definition is the one that has wide usage in conspiracy theories, which allege that the failure to peg "worthless" paper money to a commodity with intrinsic value is part of what deprives ordinary citizens of their wealth. According to these standard usages, Bitcoin could *only* be fiat money; Schroeder (2015, 1n2) writes that Bitcoin "can be considered a fiat currency in that it also has no underlying asset." Yet because of the appeal of currencies with intrinsic value to the right wing, one of the most frequent objects of Bitcoin discourse has been either to redefine "fiat" so as to exclude Bitcoin (see, e.g., both Kelly 2015; and Cox 2013 for this sort of ad-hoc redefinition), or to redefine "intrinsic value" so that some aspect of the Bitcoin software system (e.g., the energy put into mining, or the "trust" put into the system by its users) can qualify.

The supposed problem with fiat currency, which happens to be a favored talking point of conspiratorial libertarians like Ron Paul and Rand Paul (Shoff 2012), is that it interferes with the store of value function of money. Without the stability of value that they (erroneously) claim proceeds from either the use of valuable commodities as currency (e.g., gold used for coinage) or as a grounding mechanism for money (e.g., a "gold standard"), not just economic instability but actual totalitarian political power is the inevitable result. As Ron Paul put it in 2003 in a speech before the U.S. House of Representatives, "If unchecked, the economic and political chaos that comes from currency destruction inevitably leads to tyranny."

What people like Paul criticize about "fiat" currencies is that "central bankers" can manipulate the value of the currency, which is purportedly not the case with asset-backed currencies like gold. The whole point of this is to have a stable currency, one whose value does not fluctuate wildly. But because the value of Bitcoin cannot be modulated except by market transactions, it cannot separate its asset from currency functions. This makes it *too volatile* to use as a store of value, despite the fact that advocates recommend it for its superior stability.

These paradoxes are endemic to right-wing rhetoric about money, much of which encourages pushes people to abandon national moneys and to put the proceeds in precious metals like gold (see, e.g., Mencimer 2010 on Glenn Beck's promotion of gold), because they are supposedly stable in value. Yet history shows that gold standards themselves are regulatory in nature, and no more free from manipulation, derivation, and speculation than are any other currencies; gold itself provides clear evidence of this in its recent price volatility (see

Allen 2013; also see Andolfatto 2013 on the parallels between Bitcoin and gold price volatility), as do the wildly fluctuating prices of all rare commodities.

As Bitcoin hit an all-time high (albeit briefly) of US$1,124.76 on November 29, 2013 ("History of Bitcoin"), it wasn't hard to find—in fact it was difficult to avoid—cyberlibertarian believers celebrating this surge and similar ones in the past as proof of Bitcoin's importance (see, e.g., Falkvinge 2013b). While the surge certainly did indicate *something*, it was remarkable to read celebrations of the surge as if it demonstrated Bitcoin's feasibility as what it is advertised to be, a new form of money or currency. Under any conventional economic theory such surges prove not that Bitcoin is a new government-toppling currency, but to the contrary, that it *cannot* perform those functions: it is too volatile to serve as a store of value, and this function is critical to money. Like so many other aspects of cyberlibertarian practice, the case for Bitcoin's supposed power is so perched on contradictions that it is surprising to find people taking it seriously, and yet if anything exposure of these contradictions seems only to inspire renewed seriousness and missionary zeal on the part of Bitcoin advocates.

The tension between its function as currency and as investment have informed Bitcoin discussions from the beginning, but particularly in the wake of its extreme volatility during and after 2013. In the early stages of one of its surges upward in price, Pirate Party founder and self-described "political evangelist" Rick Falkvinge (2013b) posted a piece on his widely read Falkvinge.net blog titled "The Target Value for Bitcoin Is Not Some $50 or $100: It is $100,000 to $1,000,000." Falkvinge appends his Bitcoin pieces with a note saying that he "has a significant investment in Bitcoin. Specifically, he went all-in two years ago after having run these very numbers," referring to his statement in May 2011 that he was "putting all of [his] savings into Bitcoin" (Falkvinge 2011). In that earlier piece he makes the typically paradoxical claim that Bitcoin "is a currency, but an entirely new kind of currency," and then explains that he is "investing all of the money [he] had saved and all that [he] can borrow into the currency." In both pieces and many like them, Falkvinge appears unaware that he is simultaneously advocating for two diametrically opposed ends: for Bitcoin's wide adoption as money, for which it must be able to maintain a stable valuation, and for its desirability as a get-rich-quick investment, which disqualifies it as money. It is no surprise that in the same piece where Falkvinge (2011) claims that Bitcoin "will replace the current financial system" he notes that "in the past fourteen months, the value has more than thousandfolded" and predicts that in "the coming years . . . the value of a Bitcoin will increase another thousandfold" without even a hint of acknowledgment that such increases by definition would rule out Bitcoin as a form of money.

Perhaps even more remarkably, in the same piece Falkvinge claims that Bitcoin can "safeguard fundamental civil liberties for the whole population," while simultaneously noting that the "second wave" of Bitcoin adopters will be "people who don't want or are not allowed to use the legacy banking system for their everyday transactions." Since many of the regulatory measures built into the legacy banking system exist specifically to *protect* what most of us would regard as core civil liberties (e.g., to have our ownership of our property protected by deposit insurance and credit card chargebacks) the idea that Bitcoin protects civil liberties by encouraging those who are "not allowed to use the legacy banking system"—a category that mostly includes people convicted of illegal activities—is one that only a deeply committed ideologue would make.

The comparison with gold opens the door to the right-wing theories that underlie too much writing and thinking about Bitcoin. Many of its most vociferous advocates rely on characterizations of the Federal Reserve as a corrupt idea in and of itself, a device run by conspiratorial bankers who want "the state to control everyone's lives" (Weiner 2013). These claims are grounded in rhetoric propounded in the United States and across the world by far-right politicians like Ron Paul, a vocal advocate of Bitcoin (Borchgrevink 2014), whose bald declarations about the Federal Reserve are far more ideological than substantive in nature. Paul claims to want the abolition of the Fed and a return to the gold standard, as if this would result in the kind of absolute economic freedom libertarians demand, which is itself a line of argument with deep connections to racist conspiracy theories in which Paul has long been implicated (see, e.g., "Ron Paul Sites" 2011).

Such beliefs require one to ignore the direct evidence of one's own eyes. Precisely because it is outside of legal regulatory structures, Bitcoin is particularly prone to the kinds of hoarding, dumping, derivation, and manipulation that characterize all instruments that lack central bank control and regulatory oversight by bodies like the SEC. Contrary to the advocates' claims, unregulated securities instruments are everywhere in contemporary finance; there is convincing evidence that the inability of the Commodities Futures Trade Commission to establish regulatory authority over CDOs and CMOs is the proximate cause for the economic crisis of 2008 (*Frontline* 2009). Now the lack of regulation of Bitcoin means that hoarders (as of December 2013, half of all Bitcoins were owned by approximately 927 people, with such proletarian heroes as the Winklevoss twins of Facebook infamy among them; see Wile 2013) can use all sorts of sophisticated trading methods to manipulate the market. This means that fly-by-night operations can come and go, stealing huge amounts of Bitcoin for themselves, as allegedly did the operators of both the short-lived Silk Road drug supermarket replacement ironically called the Sheep Marketplace (Madore 2015) and the CEO of the most widely used Bitcoin exchange, Mt. Gox (Sarkar 2015).

Bitcoin's incredible volatility and lack of regulation, celebrated by cyberlibertarians, actually prevent the cryptocurrency from being used in just the way its advocates claim. The very reason central banks regulate the value of currencies is to ensure they serve as stable sources of value. The Bitcoin experiment demonstrates an enduring principle of finance: absolutely free markets produce extreme boom-and-bust cycles. If Bitcoin becomes regulated enough to serve as a stable store of value and to ensure that debacles like Mt. Gox don't happen in the future, it may be useful as a global system of payments (but so are generally non-transformative technologies like PayPal and Dwolla). But that will hardly shake world political structures at their foundations. If it remains outside of all forms of both value and transactional regulation, Bitcoin will continue to be a very dangerous place for any but the most risk-tolerant among us (i.e., the very wealthy, whose interest in Bitcoin should indicate to advocates how and why it cannot be economically transformative) to put their hard-earned money.

It is beyond ironic, indeed it is symptomatic, that Bitcoin has experienced dramatic deflationary and inflationary spirals just as it is being promoted as a corrective to inflation and deflation. Politically, this points to the resistance of ideologies to being disproven by contrary facts. Practically, it shows that the problems with currencies actually aren't formal, or mechanical, or algorithmic, despite what Bitcoin propagandists want us to believe. They are social and political problems that can only be solved by political mechanisms. That is why, despite the rhetoric of Bitcoin advocates, today most national currencies are far more stable than Bitcoin will ever or can ever be.

Many economists recognize something that appears to have been beyond the inventors and advocates of Bitcoin. Without direct supply-based regulatory structures that discourage an instrument from being used as an investment (aka "hoarding"), any financial instrument (even gold) will be subject to derivation, securitization, and ultimately extreme boom-and-bust cycles that it is actually the purpose of central banks to prevent. In fact, there is an underlying general proposition that applies not just to Bitcoin but also to other tradeable commodities: "investment" and "currency" functions oppose each other. Despite this, it becomes increasingly clear that a majority of Bitcoin enthusiasm emerges not from its utility as a currency but as a highly speculative investment (Glaser et al. 2014), despite the arguments in its favor focusing almost exclusively on Bitcoin's currency-like characteristics.

In fact, because the cycles of rapid deflation and inflation provoke constant exchanges of Bitcoin for other stores of value, usually national currencies, Bitcoin can more readily be understood not merely as a commodity, as just one among many other digital commodities, but also as a kind of derivative itself—an option or futures contract related to the value of other instruments and on which investors of all sorts can speculate and, depending on the volume of transactions, even manipulate the market. Given Bitcoin's foundational anti-legal regulatory stance, it is almost inconceivable that major players are refraining from such manipulation. No less a prominent Bitcoin advocate than Rick Falkvinge himself, who after claiming in March 2013 (Falkvinge 2013b) that the correct price of one Bitcoin could eventually be as high as US$1 million, wrote in September of the same year (2013a) that its valuation had become "unwarranted by several orders of magnitude" due to "illegal price-fixing," even though "for many Bitcoin enthusiasts, the Bitcoin market's unenforceability of governmental rules is a *feature,* not a bug" and that in manipulating the market, some Bitcoin traders were engaging in "cheating of some kind, a breaking of the social contract." Thus the involvement of high-profile players like the Winklevoss twins, too, cannot be a cause for celebration of Bitcoin's potential as a currency, but rather demonstrates its utility as a commodity that established capital can readily manipulate to its own ends. In this sense, it becomes a tool for existing power to concentrate itself, rather than a challenge to the existing order: as some better economically informed commentators consistently point out, Bitcoin functions much more like a speculative investment than a currency (Worstall 2013; Yermack 2014), although what one is investing in, beyond Bitcoin itself, is not at all clear.

6. The Future of Bitcoin and the Blockchain

BITCOIN IS NOT SO MUCH a single software program as it is software written using a *model* called the blockchain that is can be used to build other very similar programs (related cryptocurrencies like Litecoin, Dogecoin, and so on), but also less similar ones. The cryptographically enabled distributed ledger, and the blockchain used to implement it, advocates insist, have wide application outside of their current uses.[1] We hear (not infrequently) that the blockchain is as revolutionary today as were "personal computers in 1975, the internet in 1993" (Andreessen 2014). Networks built on such technologies are *formally* decentralized, we are told, in a way that the current internet is not, and thus allow a new range of services and opacity to oversight (and therefore legal as well as unlawful surveillance). Of course, in many ways "centralized" and "decentralized" are metaphors, and also adjectives

---

1. For thoughtful and critical overviews of blockchain technology viewed separately from Bitcoin, see DuPont and Maurer (2015) and Grimmelmann and Narayanan (2016). Typically hype-filled presentations include Naughton (2016), Swan (2015), and Tapscott and Tapscott (2016).

that can apply to many different parts of systems. Facebook, for example, might be seen as decentralized because it is made up of its millions of users, spread out all over the planet; as centralized, because one company collects all of the data from those users; as decentralized, because all that data is not housed in a single geographic location, but on servers all over the world; as centralized, because those locations are nevertheless tightly held together via software and hardware; and on and on. The valorization of "decentralization" as a good in itself too often obscures as much as it reveals (Galloway 2014; Golumbia 2012), and there are any number of ways in which, despite its technically decentralized nature, Bitcoin functions as a centralized and concentrated locus of financial power (see, e.g., Wile 2013).

Advocates are right that it is difficult to grasp the potential uses of such networks without seeing them in action, but on the surface they seem structured around promises that appeal to and reinforce rightist political ideologies. These are almost exclusively ideologies that are broadly libertarian in character. They follow Friedrich Hayek and his disciple Jimmy Wales in believing that markets (see Mirowski 2014, 82–83), not formal political structures, are the only valid means for power to be wielded, and that "the good will out" if we impose competitive market structures over parts of society, like the issuance of money, that governments have claimed as part of their domain. Despite their frequent invocation of "democratization," such efforts are profoundly antidemocratic, insisting that the introduction of devices and software by a self-identified technocratic elite trumps duly enacted laws and law enforcement mechanisms, and that a kind of market—a market in adoption of such services—is the exclusive method society should use to judge the provision of these services. The most fervent advocates of such strategies are open in their rejection of democratic governance: "'We see this as part of the total sublation of the state,' said Cody Wilson . . . who gained fame earlier this year when he published online the blueprints to a pistol that could be manufactured with a 3D printer. 'I know I sound like some kind of weird Jehovah's Witness, but we've only just begun. We admit that we are ideologues'" (Feuer 2013).[2] There was a time when it might have been relatively difficult to imagine a software platform that had more power as a politics than in its practical applications; it also used to be hard to imagine right-wing extremists like Cody Wilson being quoted as authoritative about anything in our nation's leading newspapers. It is an index of Bitcoin's power as ideology (and of the power of that ideology itself) that today such statements pass without much notice, and it is no less an index of the threat such technologies, and even more so, the ideologies they embody, pose to democracy itself.[3] It is a threat the advocates of such technologies themselves frequently advertise, and it is this feature of cryptocurrencies and blockchain technologies that all non-rightist political thinkers need to take seriously.

Part of what makes Bitcoin such an intriguing cultural phenomenon is that while its proponents are firmly convinced of its success, they have serious difficulty agreeing about what that success would be. On the one hand, because Bitcoin is sup-

2. For background on Cody Wilson and his promotion of 3D-printed guns, see Silverman (2013).

3. Some of the few exceptions to this rule in scholarship—political analysis that acknowledges the parallels or connections between Bitcoin discourse and far-right political beliefs—include Maurer, Nelms, and Swartz (2013), Payne (2013), and Scott (2014). Robinson (2014) is the best introduction to the general system of beliefs found among Bitcoin promoters.

posed to replace the currencies of corrupt central banks, success means widespread adoption of Bitcoin. But "widespread adoption" inherently includes adoption by the very bankers, financiers, and politicians some Bitcoin enthusiasts loathe so much, and therefore signs of widespread adoption are taken as unfortunate corruptions of the Bitcoin ideal. In another register, Bitcoin is supposed to "end the nation-state," or at least the nation-state's "tyranny" over money, goals toward which its widespread adoption is supposed to lead; so as Bitcoin does in fact become more widely adopted, but with virtually no impact on either the nation-state or reserve banking, it is seen as a disappointing failure. The dream of Bitcoin ubiquity is one of total social transformation, in the direction of extreme anarcho-capitalism. Therefore it is possible to suggest both that Bitcoin will succeed and is succeeding, and that yet this success will not satisfy the demands of the most fervent Bitcoin advocates (for such contradictory assertions see, e.g., both Ito 2016; and Redman 2016; for the difficulty of defining "success" in Bitcoin, see both Hearn 2016; and the discussion of it in the various Bitcoin communities). Bitcoin as ideology will go on to find itself even more extreme instantiations, which may or may not manifest its overt political goals. Regardless of whether Bitcoin realizes these goals, its primary social function is to spread these ideas and give them more widespread legitimacy than John Birch Society pamphlets ever did.

Pushed to its limit, Bitcoin revels in contradictions that only committed ideologues could think reasonable. Jeffrey Tucker—an avowed anarcho-capitalist, "Chief Liberty Officer and founder of Liberty.me," and right-wing Heartland Institute policy adviser—is one of the most strident promoters of cyberlibertarian ideology and of Bitcoin and blockchain technology. Tucker's use of the language of "peer-to-peer" and "sharing" (in particular Tucker 2015a) along with his relentless disparagement of democratic governance should give all non-right-wing digital enthusiasts pause. Bitcoin and its associated exchanges and services have been thoroughly implicated in scams and manipulation of every sort (for just a partial list through the end of 2014 see "List of Bitcoin Heists"). In part this stems from the deliberate design of Bitcoin to prevent legal regulation. It also tells us a lot about the way people behave when they believe they are outside or above the rule of law, especially when money is involved. In a bizarre piece called "A Theory of the Scam" (Tucker 2015b), Tucker explains away these scams and thefts, which on most non-extremist accounts emerge directly from Bitcoin's hostility toward legal regulation, advising his readers, "Never think that the presence of rackets in an industry discredits that industry."

Tucker notes, not without some basis in fact, that enormous industries and world-transforming technologies like the printing press and railroads were rife with scams in their early days, although he fails to demonstrate that these histories truly are parallel with what we see today with Bitcoin. Tucker's philosophical argument is even more remarkable: "Why are scam artists so attracted to Bitcoin? The answer is actually flattering. Scam artists are the evil cousins of genuine entrepreneurs. They are alert to new opportunities. They are attracted to ventures that are popular among the smart set. They are profoundly aware of what people imagine to be the next big thing. Where there is opportunity and the prospect of high profits, there are scammers. Their interest in Bitcoin, then, is actually a bullish sign. I would be more worried about this market if scam artists were not interested in it." All one has to do is to consider the extensive history of "technologies" and products that were nothing but scams—to say nothing of the many products that have developed without much of a history of scamming at all—to see how self-serving this argument is. If the presence of scams is an indication of the health of a given product or technology, then cold fusion, patent medicine, unregulated mutual funds (the kind that were shut down in the midst of the financial crises of the 1920s and 1930s), and penny stocks should all be excellent candidates for safe and successful investment.

Tucker's argument, while it may be an especially pointed and telling version, is one that we find repeatedly in Bitcoin advocacy. Despite the fact that, compared with other technologies, other currencies, and other forms of payment, Bitcoin's resistance to legal oversight makes it ripe for misuse and abuse of all sorts, its advocates portray that resistance as the most important kind of "freedom," in no small part because they benefit from blurring the lines between legal and illegal, scam and legitimate transaction, and because they are committed to a highly attenuated and specific notion of "freedom." The whole point of the enterprise, as with most of the efforts promoted by libertarians and anarcho-capitalists, is to enable a wide range of extractive and exploitative business practices, and thus to increase the power of corporations and capital outside the scope of any attempts by democratic polities to constrain them.

Among the most suggestive of the proposed alternate uses for the blockchain is in the creation of what advocates variously refer to as a "Decentralized Autonomous Organization" (DAO) or "Decentralized Autonomous Corporation" (DAC). One early promoter of what he calls "Bitcoin as platform" describes them this way: "Bitcoin is the first prototype of a real decentralized autonomous corporation (DAC), where the Bitcoin holders are the equity shareholders of Bitcoin Inc. Stan Larimer, president of Invictus Innovations, defines a DAC as follows: 'Distributed Autonomous Corporations (DAC) run without any human involvement under the control of an incorruptible set of business rules. (That's why they must be distributed and autonomous.) These rules are implemented as publicly auditable open source software distributed across the computers of their stakeholders'" (Duivestein 2015). At some level this appears reasonable, but it turns out to be anything but clear exactly what DACs or DAOs are supposed to be or do. One of the simplest illustrations has to do with what advocates call "smart contracts": "A smart contract is the simplest form of decentralized automation, and is most easily and accurately defined as follows: a smart contract is a mechanism involving digital assets and two or more parties, where some or all of the parties put assets in and assets are automatically redistributed among those parties according to a formula based on certain data that is not known at the time the contract is initiated" (Buterin 2014). The point is that the contract, once agreed to by both parties, fulfills itself when the conditions have been met, without the parties needing to take additional action. The contract is "decentralized" (it does not exist in any one specific location) and "autonomous" (it works on its own without the intervention of other agents).

Advocates for DAOs, DACs and their offshoots spend a great deal of time, unsurprisingly, on describing the technology that might allow these structures to come into being. But as with Bitcoin itself, it is hard not to see—that is, if one is looking for it—the extremist assumptions on which the notions of DAOs and DACs and their ilk are built. One of the main proponents of DAOs and DACs is Vitalik Buterin, author of the passage about "smart contracts" above, "a Canadian college dropout and Bitcoin enthusiast" (Schneider 2014), cofounder of *Bitcoin Magazine,* and a recipient of one of the US$100,000 Thiel Fellowships funded by the eponymous right-wing technology entrepreneur and PayPal founder Peter Thiel (Rizzo 2014a)— fellowships that specifically promote the rejection of higher education, in a manner harmonious with the rejection by

Thiel and others on the right wing of public goods (Lind 2014). Buterin is a cofounder of Ethereum, the best-known project to generalize blockchain technology into applications that go beyond currency-like systems.

Buterin (2014) describes DAOs "and their subclass, DACs," as the "holy grail" of decentralized applications. A DAO "is an entity that lives on the internet and exists autonomously, but also heavily relies on hiring individuals to perform certain tasks that the automaton itself cannot do." While a DAO is "not an artificial intelligence," it "makes decisions for itself." A DAO has "internal capital . . . [it] contains some kind of internal property that is valuable in some way, and it has the ability to use that property as a mechanism for rewarding certain activities." Exactly what these DAOs will do or could do remains fuzzy, but it is hard not to notice that the representation most frequently picked by DAO *advocates* for what a real DAO would look like is the "Daemon" process described by science fiction author and IT consultant Daniel Suarez in his novels *Daemon* (2006) and *Freedom™* (2010). In Suarez's books, the "Daemon" is a set of autonomous algorithms designed by a genius-level software developer and set to begin running when he dies. The "Daemon" that is thereby unleashed, while not itself possessing any sort of will or desire, carries out a complex series of conditional orders that ultimately result in a complete global revolution: it resembles, though it is not, an "evil genius" bent on global power, one who centralizes and concentrates power in itself and in those it deems to be worthy subordinates (many people in the world of the novels think that some living person or group of persons is behind the "Daemon's" actions, although readers know that this is not the case). Despite the revolution having some positive aspects, it is hard to read these books and see Suarez as having any goal other than to show the malevolent intent and dangerous potential of such autonomous and uncontrollable algorithms with capital. Yet blockchain promoters take the books as portraying a desirable outcome and frequently invoke the Daemon as the thing they are attempting to build (see, e.g., "Decentralized Autonomous Corporation"; Duivestein 2015; Swan 2015, 17), without noting the apocalyptic character of Suarez's novel.

The close tie between capital and the ideas of DAOs and DACs shows the remarkable way in which, despite the rhetoric of revolution and "democratization," what these structures offer is an even further intensification of the power of capital to escape legal and democratic oversight. The terminological play at work in the DAO and DAC names already discloses something of the built-in and highly questionable assumptions on which the projects themselves are based: that loci of concentrated power are currently "centralized" and not "autonomous," so that what is needed are their opposites. Yet it is hard to see how a dispassionate observer of contemporary political economy could agree with such an assessment: to the contrary, many of the most serious economic and political problems today emerge just from the ability of concentrations of capital, usually under the name of "corporations," to act in a remarkably decentralized and autonomous fashion. One might say without exaggeration that the last thing the world needs is the granting to capital of even more power, independent of democratic oversight, than it has already taken for itself.

Bitcoin enthusiasts have an uncanny ability to interpret every event as an indicator of the inevitable "success" of the cryptocurrency. When Bitcoin's value relative to world currencies goes up, enthusiasts celebrate; when it goes down, it is a mark of a coming stability that augurs success as a store of value, despite there being historical precedent only contrary to this development. Regulation that enables Bitcoin trade means the currency is being taken seriously; regulation that restricts trade means that governments are failing and the "new" Bitcoin economy is rising to replace it. This pattern itself is one of the strongest indicators of Bitcoin's ideological power, which is reflected no less in the structure of the blockchain itself as it is in the discourse that surrounds it.

Paradoxically, then, the fact that venture capitalists are reputed to have invested widely in companies focused in some way or another on Bitcoin is a sign of both mainstream adoption and the destruction of the "mainstream." At this point it is certainly absolutely possible that many retailers may come to accept Bitcoin as a medium of exchange, and major retailers like Amazon, Target, and Dell already accept it at least to some extent. Yet such success disappoints at some level, because simply having one more option among many others to pay for things seems anything but revolutionary. Further, the inherent fluctuations in value and the costs involved with exchanging Bitcoin for other, more widely accepted exchange instruments end up mitigating some of Bitcoin's purported strengths. Exchange fees typically mirror the middleman transaction fees Bitcoin enthusiasts dislike so much (Kroeger and Sarkar 2016), and the reversibility of credit card and some bank transactions is for most users a feature rather than a bug. In general, to most users, other systems of exchange have benefits Bitcoin explicitly rejects, and the more Bitcoin enthusiasts realize how important these benefits are, the less revolutionary and transformational it appears. So the likelihood of widespread use appears in somewhat inverse proportion to its "revolutionary" potential: the more widely used it is, the less it seems to mean.

Yet this should not defuse concerns about Bitcoin's potential (and that of the blockchain), both as platform and as politics. In fact, it's not clear which is more worrisome. As objects of discourse, Bitcoin and the blockchain do a remarkable job of reinforcing the view that the entire global history of political thought and action needs to be jettisoned, or, even worse, that it has *already been* jettisoned through the introduction of any number of digital technologies. Thus, in the introduction to a bizarrely earnest and destructive volume called *From Bitcoin to Burning Man and Beyond* (Clippinger and Bollier 2014), the editors, one of whom is a research scientist at MIT, write, "Enlightenment ideals of democratic rule seem to have run their course. A continuous flow of scientific findings are undermining many foundational claims about human rationality and perfectibility while exponential technological changes and exploding global demographics overwhelm the capacity of democratic institutions to rule effectively, and ultimately, their very legitimacy" (x). Such abrupt dismissals of hundreds of years of thought, work, and lives follows directly from cyberlibertarian thought and extremist reinterpretations of political institutions: "What once required the authority of a central bank or a sovereign authority can now be achieved through open, distributed crypto-algorithms. National borders, traditional legal regimes, and human intervention are increasingly moot" (xi). Like most ideological formations, these sentiments are highly resistant to being proven false by facts. Thus, when Bitcoin faced a technical issue over the size of the blocks that make up the blockchain, a problem that could eventually result in the entire blockchain becoming unstable or too slow to process transactions, a fight broke out about the possible shift to a new version (in open source software development terms, a "fork") of the software. In the course of the fight a rift was revealed between the two individuals with full access to the Bitcoin code, who developed and supported the fork, and others who opposed it (Bustillos 2015). These are problems of governance, authority, and centralization, and rather than a decentralized, super-democratic, and distributed governance mechanism revealing its efficacy, even Bitcoin's own governance structures displayed exactly the autocracy, infighting, bad faith, and centralization that the blockchain is often said to have magically dissolved.

Few attitudes typify the paradoxical cyberlibertarian mind-set of Bitcoin promoters (and many others) more than do those of "Sanjuro," the alias of the person who created a Bitcoin "assassination market" (Greenberg 2013). Sanjuro believes that by incentivizing people to kill politicians, he will destroy "all governments, everywhere." This anarchic apocalypse "will change the world for the better," producing "a world without wars, dragnet Panopticon-style surveillance, nuclear weapons, armies, repression, money manipulation, and limits to trade." Only someone so blinkered by their ideological tunnel vision could look at world history and imagine that murdering the representatives of democratically elected governments and thus putting the governments themselves out of existence would do anything but make every one of these problems immeasurably worse than they already are. Yet this, in the end, is the extreme rightist—anarcho-capitalist, winner-take-all, even neo-feudalist—political vision too many of those in the Bitcoin (along with other cryptocurrency) and blockchain communities, whatever they believe their political orientation to be, are working actively to bring about. This is not to say that Bitcoin and the blockchain can never be used for non-rightist purposes, and even less that everyone in the blockchain communities is on the right. Yet it is hard to see how this minority can resist the political values that are very literally coded into the software itself. Recent events have shown repeatedly that we discount the power of engineers and/or ideologues to realize their political visions through software design at our peril. What is required to combat that power is not more wars between algorithmic platforms and individuals who see themselves as above politics, but a reassertion of the political power that the blockchain is specifically constructed to dismantle.

Acknowledgments

I appreciate helpful comments on earlier versions of this manuscript from Mark Ames, Quinn DuPont, Arne DeBoever, Frank Pasquale, and an anonymous reader from the University of Minnesota Press. Conversations with Dale Carrico, Primavera De Filippi, Trevor Kroger, Yasha Levine, Geert Lovink, Rachel O'Dwyer, Nathaniel Tkacz, and the audience at the Money Lab 2: Economies of Dissent conference contributed to the final shape of the argument. I am particularly grateful to Lisa Alspector for her extensive editorial comments.

Bibliography

Abel, Andrew B., Ben S. Bernanke, and Dean Croushore. 2008.
   Macroeconomics. 3rd ed. Boston: Pearson.

Allen, Katie. 2013. "Gold Price Volatility Hits Pawnbroker's Profits."
   The Guardian (September). http://www.theguardian.com/.

Ames, Mark. 2015. "Google Is Helping to Fund the Group That's Trying
   to Kill Obamacare in the Supreme Court." *Pando Daily* (March 18).
   http://pando.com/.

Andolfatto, David. 2013. "Why Gold and Bitcoin Make Lousy Money."
   Economist's View (April). http://economistsview.typepad.com.

Andreessen, Marc. 2014. "Why Bitcoin Matters." *New York Times*
   (January). http://dealbook.nytimes.com/.

Antonopoulos, Andreas M. 2014. *Mastering Bitcoin*. Sebastopol, Calif.:
   O'Reilly Media.

Aziz, John. 2013. "Is Inflation Always and Everywhere a Monetary
   Phenomenon?" Azizonomics (March 10). http://azizonomics.com/.

———. 2014. "Why Won't Inflation Conspiracy Theories Just Die
   Already?" *The Week* (August 14). http://theweek.com/.

Barbrook, Richard, and Andy Cameron. 1996. "The Californian
   Ideology." *Science as Culture* 6, no. 1: 44–72.

Barlow, John Perry. 1996. "A Declaration of the Independence of
   Cyberspace." Electronic Frontier Foundation. http://projects
   .eff.org/.

Bauwens, Michel. 2014. "A Political Evaluation of Bitcoin." P2P
   Foundation (September 9). https://blog.p2pfoundation.net/.

Beigel, Ofir. 2015. "On Mixers, Tumblers, and Bitcoin Pseudonymity."
   Bytecoin (June 10). http://bytecoin.org/.

Berlet, Chip. 2009. *Toxic to Democracy: Conspiracy Theories, Demonization, and Scapegoating*. Somerville, Mass.: Political Research Associates.

Berlet, Chip, and Matthew N. Lyons. 2000. *Right-Wing Populism in America: Too Close for Comfort*. New York: Guilford Press.

Berlin, Isaiah. 1958. "Two Concepts of Liberty." In *Liberty*, 166–217. New York: Oxford University Press, 2002.

Birchall, Clare. 2006. *Knowledge Goes Pop: From Conspiracy Theory to Gossip*. Oxford, UK: Berg.

Boase, Richard. 2013. "Cypherpunks, Bitcoin, and the Myth of Satoshi Nakamoto." Cybersalon (September 5). http://www.cybersalon.org/.

Borchgrevink, Jonas. 2014. "Ron Paul Loves His Own Ron Paul Coin and Is Positive about Bitcoin." CryptoCoinsNews (January 16). http://www.cryptocoinsnews.com/.

Brands, H. W. 2006. *The Money Men: Capitalism, Democracy, and the Hundred Years' War over the American Dollar*. New York: Norton.

Bratich, Jack Z. 2008. *Conspiracy Panics: Political Rationality and Popular Culture*. Albany: State University of New York Press.

Brito, Jerry, and Andrea Castillo. 2013. *Bitcoin: A Primer for Policymakers*. Arlington, Va.: Mercatus Center, George Mason University.

Brown, Ellen Hodgson. 2008. *Web of Debt: The Shocking Truth about Our Money System and How We Can Break Free*. 3rd ed. Baton Rouge, La.: Third Millennium Press.

Bustillos, Maria. 2015. "Inside the Fight over Bitcoin's Future." *New Yorker* (August 25). http://www.newyorker.com/.

Burdekin, Richard C., and Pierre L. Siklos, eds. 2004. *Deflation: Current and Historical Perspectives*. New York: Cambridge University Press.

Buterin, Vitalik. 2014. "DAOs, DACs, Das, and More: An Incomplete Terminology Guide." Ethereum (May 6). http://blog.ethereum.org/.

Carrico, Dale. 2005. "Pancryptics: Technocultural Transformations of the Subject of Privacy." Ph.D. diss., University of California, Berkeley.

——. 2009. "Condensed Critique of Transhumanism." Amor Mundi (January 25). http://amormundi.blogspot.com/.

——. 2013a. "Futurological Discourse and Posthuman Terrains." *Existenz* 8, no. 2: 47–63.

——. 2013b. "The Superlative Summary." Amor Mundi (July 14). http://amormundi.blogspot.com/.

Casey, Michael J. 2014. "Bitcoin Foundation's Chief Jon Matonis to Resign." *Wall Street Journal* (October 30). http://www.wsj.com/.

Chomsky, Noam. 2015. "Creating the Horror Chamber." *Jacobin* (July 28). http://www.jacobinmag.com/.

Clippinger, John H., and David Bollier, eds. 2014. *From Bitcoin to Burning Man and Beyond: The Quest for Identity and Autonomy in a Digital Society.* Boston: ID3 / Off the Common Books.

Conner, Claire. 2013. *Wrapped in the Flag: What I Learned Growing Up in America's Radical Right, How I Escaped, and Why My Story Matters Today.* Boston: Beacon Press.

"Controlled Supply." Bitcoin wiki. http://en.bitcoin.it/.

Cox, James. 2013. *Bitcoin and Digital Currencies: The New World of Money and Freedom.* Baltimore: Laissez Faire Books.

Davidson, Paul. 2013. "Is Bitcoin 'Money'? The Post-Keynesian View." Real-World Economics Review Blog (November), http://rwer.wordpress.com/.

"Decentralized Autonomous Corporation." Coinwiki. http://coinwiki.info/.

Diamond, Sara. 1995. *Roads to Dominion: Right-Wing Movements and Political Power in the United States.* New York: Guilford Press.

Doherty, Brian. 1995. "The Best of Both Worlds: An Interview with Milton Friedman." *Reason* (June 1). http://reason.com/

Duivestein, Sander. 2015. "Bitcoin 2.0 Enables Autonomous, Leaderless Organizations." Sogeti Labs (March 12). http://labs.sogeti.com/.

Duivestein, Sander, and Patrick Savalle. 2014. "Bitcoin 2.0: It's the Platform, Not the Currency, Stupid!" SlideShare. http://www.slideshare.net/patricksavalle/.

DuPont, Quinn. 2014. "The Politics of Cryptography: Bitcoin and the Ordering Machines." *Journal of Peer Production* 4 (January). http://peerproduction.net/.

DuPont, Quinn, and Bill Maurer. 2015. "Ledgers and Law in the Blockchain." *King's Review* (June 23). http://kingsreview.co.uk/.

Dyson, Esther, George Gilder, George Keyworth, and Alvin Toffler. 1994. "Cyberspace and the American Dream: A Magna Carta for the Knowledge Age." *Future Insight* (August). http://www.pff.org/.

Emery, Joel, and Miranda Stewart. 2015. "All around the World, Regulators Are Realizing Bitcoin Is Money." The Conversation (August 11). http://theconversation.com/.

Epperson, A. Ralph. 1985. *The Unseen Hand: An Introduction to the Conspiratorial View of History.* Tucson: Publius Press.

Falkvinge, Rick. 2011. "Why I'm Putting All My Savings into Bitcoin." Falkvinge.net (May 29). http://falkvinge.net/.

———. 2013a. "Bitcoin's Vast Overvaluation Appears Partially Caused by (Usually) Illegal Price-Fixing." Falkvinge.net (September 13). http://falkvinge.net/.

———. 2013b. "The Target Value for Bitcoin Is Not Some $50 or $100: It is $100,000 to $1,000,000." Falkvinge.net (March 6). http://falkvinge.net/.

Farivar, Cyrus. 2013. "Federal Reserve: While Bitcoins Hold 'Promise,' We Have No Regulatory Authority." Ars Technica (November 18). http://arstechnica.com/.

Federal Reserve Bank of St. Louis. 2015a. "A Closer Look at Open Market Operations." Federal Reserve Bank of St. Louis. http://www.stlouisfed.org/.

———. 2015b. "How Monetary Policy Works." Federal Reserve Bank of St. Louis. http://www.stlouisfed.org/.

Felten, Ed. 2014. "Bitcoin Mining Now Dominated by One Pool." Freedom to Tinker (June 16). http://freedom-to-tinker.com/.

Feuer, Alan. 2013. "The Bitcoin Ideology." *New York Times* (December). http://www.nytimes.com/.

Flanders, Laura, ed. 2010. *At the Tea Party: The Wing Nuts, Whack Jobs, and Whitey-Whiteness of the New Republican Right . . . and Why We Should Take It Seriously.* New York: OR Books.

Foxman, Simone. 2012. "Ron Paul Believes in an Inflation Conspiracy Theory: And Here's Why It's Totally Wrong." *Business Insider* (February 29). http://www.businessinsider.com/.

Friedman, Milton. 1963. "Inflation: Causes and Consequences." In Friedman, *Dollars and Deficits: Inflation, Monetary Policy, and the Balance of Payments*, 21–71. Englewood Cliffs, N.J.: Prentice-Hall, 1968.

———. 1993. *Why Government Is the Problem*. Stanford, Calif.: Hoover Institution Press.

Frisby, Dominic. 2014. *Bitcoin: The Future of Money?* London: Unbound.

Frisch, Helmut. 1983. *Theories of Inflation*. New York: Cambridge University Press.

Frontline. 2009. "Interview with Brooksley Born." (October). PBS. http://www.pbs.org/wgbh/pages/frontline/.

Galbraith, John Kenneth. 1975. *Money: Whence It Came From, Where It Went*. New York: Houghton Mifflin.

Galloway, Alexander R. 2014. "The Reticular Fallacy." *The b2 Review* (December 17). http://boundary2.org/.

Gans, Joshua. 2013. "Time for a Little Bitcoin Discussion." Economist's View (December). http://economistsview.typepad.com/.

Giddens, Anthony. 1985. *The Nation State and Violence*. Vol. 2 of *A Contemporary Critique of Historical Materialism*. Cambridge, UK: Polity Press.

Gillman, Howard. 1995. *The Constitution Besieged: The Rise and Demise of Lochner Era Police Powers Jurisprudence*. Durham, N.C.: Duke University Press.

Glaser, Florian, Kai Zimmermann, Martin Haferkorn, Moritz Christian Weber, and Michael Siering. 2014. "Bitcoin: Asset or Currency? Revealing Users' Hidden Intentions." Twenty Second European Conference on Information Systems. http://papers.ssrn.com/.

"Gold Fix: The London Gold Fix." BullionVault. http://www.bullionvault.com/.

Golumbia, David. 2009. *The Cultural Logic of Computation*. Cambridge, Mass.: Harvard University Press.

———. 2012. "Computerization, Centralization, and Concentration." uncomputing (October 25). http://www.uncomputing.org/.

———. 2013a. "Completely Different and Exactly the Same." uncomputing (March 6). http://www.uncomputing.org/.

———. 2013b. "Cyberlibertarianism: The Extremist Foundations of 'Digital Freedom.'" Talk delivered at Clemson University (September). http://www.uncomputing.org/.

———. 2013c. "Cyberlibertarians' Digital Deletion of the Left." *Jacobin* (December 4). http://www.jacobinmag.com/.

———. 2014a. "Bitcoinsanity 1: The (Ir)relevance of Finance, or, It's (Not) Different This Time." uncomputing (January 6). http://www.uncomputing.org/.

———. 2014b. "Bitcoinsanity 2: Revolutions in Rhetoric." uncomputing (June 26). http://www.uncomputing.org/.

———. In preparation. *Cyberlibertarianism: How the Digital Revolution Tilts Right*.

Gongloff, Mark. 2013. "Paul Krugman Trolls Bitcoin Fans: Guess What Happens Next." *Huffington Post* (December 30). http://www.huffingtonpost.com/.

Goodley, Simon. 2013. "Could Gold Be the Next Libor Scandal?" *The Guardian* (March). http://www.theguardian.com/.

Greenberg, Andy. 2013. "Meet the 'Assassination Market' Creator Who's Crowdfunding Murder with Bitcoins." *Forbes* (November). http://www.forbes.com/.

Griffin, G. Edward. 1998. *The Creature from Jekyll Island: A Second Look at the Federal Reserve.* 3rd ed. Westlake Village, Calif.: American Media.

Grimmelmann, James, and Arvind Narayanan. 2016. "The Blockchain Gang." *Slate* (February 18). http://www.slate.com/.

Hardoon, Deborah. 2015. "Wealth: Having It All and Wanting More." Oxfam Issue Report (January). http://policy-practice.oxfam.org.uk/.

Hayase, Nozomi. 2015. "Coding Freedom: Can Blockchain Technology Help Build a Foundation for Real Democracy?" Falkvinge.net (March 22). http://falkvinge.net/.

Hearn, Mike. 2016. "The Resolution of the Bitcoin Experiment." Medium (January 14). https://medium.com/@octskyward/.

Hoepman, Jaap-Henk. 2008. "Distributed Double Spending Prevention." http://arxiv.org/.

"History of Bitcoin." Wikipedia. http://en.wikipedia.org/.

"How Does Bitcoin Work?" 2015. Bitcoin.org. http://bitcoin.org/.

Hughes, Eric. 1993. "A Cypherpunk's Manifesto." Electronic Frontier Foundation. http://www.eff.org/.

Hutchinson, Frances, Mary Mellor, and Wendy Olsen. 2002. *The Politics of Money: Towards Sustainability and Economic Democracy.* London: Pluto Press.

Ingham. Geoffrey. 2004. *The Nature of Money,* Malden, Mass.: Polity Press.

Ito, Joi. 2016. "Why I'm Worried about Bitcoin and the Blockchain." CoinDesk (February 22). http://www.coindesk.com/.

John Birch Society. 2009. "What Is Money?" http://www.jbs.org/.

Kelly, Brian. 2015. *The Bitcoin Big Bang: How Alternative Currencies Are about to Change the World.* Hoboken, N.J.: Wiley.

Kostakis, Vasilis, and Chris Giotitsas. 2014. "The (A)Political Economy of Bitcoin." *TripleC: Communication, Capitalism, and Critique* 12, no. 2: 431–40.

Kroeger, Alexander, and Asani Sarkar. 2016. "Is Bitcoin Really Frictionless?" *Liberty Street Economics* (March 23). http://libertystreeteconomics.newyorkfed.org/.

Krugman, Paul. 2007. "Who Was Milton Friedman?" *New York Review of Books* (February 15). http://www.nybooks.com/.

——. 2011. "Inflation Conspiracy Theories." *New York Times* (December 18). http://krugman.blogs.nytimes.com/.

———. 2013. "Bitcoin Is Evil." *New York Times* (December 28). http://krugman.blogs.nytimes.com/.

Lanchester, John. 2016. "When Bitcoin Grows Up." *London Review of Books* 38, no. 8: 3–12.

Langlois, Jill. 2013. "Liberty Reserve Digital Money Service Shut Down, Founder Arrested." *GlobalPost* (May 27). http://www.globalpost.com/.

Larson, Martin. 1975. *The Federal Reserve and Our Manipulated Dollar: With Comments on the Causes of Wars, Depressions, Inflation, and Poverty.* Old Greenwich, Conn.: Devin-Adair.

Lepore, Jill. 2010. *The Whites of Their Eyes: The Tea Party's Revolution and the Battle over American History.* Princeton, N.J.: Princeton University Press.

Levin, Mark R. 2009. *Liberty and Tyranny: A Conservative Manifesto.* New York: Simon and Schuster.

Lind, Michael. 2014. "Why Celebrity 'Genius' Peter Thiel Is Grossly Overrated." *Salon* (September 11). http://www.salon.com/.

"List of Bitcoin Heists." 2014. Bitcointalk.org forum. http://bitcointalk.org/.

Liu, Alec. 2013. "Why Bitcoins Are Just Like Gold." *Vice Motherboard* (March 21). http://motherboard.vice.com/.

Lopp, Jameson. 2016. "Bitcoin and the Rise of the Cypherpunks." CoinDesk (April 9). http://www.coindesk.com/.

Madore, P. H. 2015. "Alleged Sheep Marketplace Owner Identified in Czech Republic." CryptoCoinsNews (March 29). http://www.cryptocoinsnews.com/.

Malcolm, Jeremy. 2013. "Internet Freedom in a World of States." Paper presented at WSIS+10 Review (February 27). http://www.intgovforum.org/.

Malmo, Christopher. 2015. "Bitcoin Is Unsustainable." *Vice Motherboard* (June 29). http://motherboard.vice.com/.

Marx, Jared Paul. 2015. "Bitcoin as a Commodity: What the CFTC's Ruling Means." CoinDesk (September 21). http://www.coindesk.com/.

Matonis, Jon. 2012a. "Bitcoin Prevents Monetary Tyranny." *Forbes* (October). http://www.forbes.com/.

———. 2012b. "WikiLeaks Bypasses Financial Blockade with Bitcoin." *Forbes* (August). http://www.forbes.com/.

Maurer, Bill, Taylor C. Nelms, and Lana Swartz. 2013. "'When Perhaps the Real Problem Is Money Itself!': The Practical Materiality of Bitcoin." *Social Semiotics* 23, no. 2: 261–77.

May, Timothy C. 1992. "The Crypto-Anarchist Manifesto." Activism
.net. http://www.activism.net/.

Meiklejohn, Sarah, and Claudio Orlandi. 2015. "Privacy-Enhancing
Overlays in Bitcoin." Financial Cryptography and Data Security
Nineteenth Annual Conference. http://fc15.ifca.ai/.

Mellor, Mary. 2010. *The Future of Money: From Financial Crisis to
Public Resource*. London: Pluto Press.

Mencimer, Stephanie. 2010. "Glenn Beck's Golden Fleece: The Right
Wing's Paranoid Pitch for Overpriced Gold." In *At the Tea Party:
The Wing Nuts, Whack Jobs, and Whitey-Whiteness of the New
Republican Right . . . and Why We Should Take It Seriously*, edited by
Laura Flanders, 247–59. New York: OR Books.

Michaels, Walter Benn. 1988. *The Gold Standard and the Logic of
Naturalism: American Literature at the Turn of the Century*.
Berkeley: University of California Press.

Mirowski, Philip. 2014. *Never Let a Serious Crisis Go to Waste: How
Neoliberalism Survived the Financial Meltdown*. New York: Verso Books.

Mishkin, Frederic S. 1984. "The Causes of Inflation." National Bureau
of Economic Research Working Paper 1453. http://www.nber.org/.

Mullins, Eustace. 1992. *The World Order: Our Secret Rulers*. Rev. ed.
Staunton, Va.: Ezra Pound Institute of Civilization.

———. 1993. *The Secrets of the Federal Reserve: The London Connection*.
Carson City, Nev.: Bridger House Press.

Mulloy, Darren. 2005. *American Extremism: History, Politics, and the
Militia Movement*. New York: Routledge.

Murray, Cameron (Rumpelstatskin). 2013. "Everything I Was Afraid to
Ask about Bitcoin but Did." Naked Capitalism (November). http://
www.nakedcapitalism.com/.

"Myths." Bitcoin wiki. http://en.bitcoin.it/.

Nakamoto, Satoshi. 2008. "Bitcoin: A Peer-to-Peer Electronic Cash
System." Bitcoin.org. http://bitcoin.org/.

———. 2009. "Bitcoin Open Source Implementation of
P2P Currency." P2P Foundation (February 11). http://
p2pfoundation.ning.com/.

Naughton, John. 2016. "Is Blockchain the Most Important IT Invention of
Our Age?" *The Guardian* (January 24). http://www.theguardian.com.

O'Dwyer, Rachel. 2015. "The Revolution Will (Not) Be Decentralized:
Blockchain-Based Technologies and the Commons." Academia.edu.
https://www.academia.edu/.

Otar, Okropir. 2015. "Mining Consolidation: The Bitcoin Guillotine?" Bitcoin News Channel (December 20). http://bitcoinnews channel.com/.

Pagliery, Jose. 2014. *Bitcoin: And the Future of Money*. Chicago: Triumph Books.

Patron, Travis. 2015. *The Bitcoin Revolution: An Internet of Money*. Diginomics.com.

Paul, Ron. 2003. "Paper Money and Tyranny." U.S. House of Representatives (September 5). Archived at https://www .lewrockwell.com/.

Payne, Alex. 2013. "Bitcoin, Magical Thinking, and Political Ideology." al3x.net (December 18). http://al3x.net/.

Perelman, Michael. 2007. *The Confiscation of American Prosperity: From Right-Wing Extremism and Economic Ideology to the Next Great Depression*. New York: Palgrave Macmillan.

Pettifor, Ann. 2014. *Just Money: How Society Can Break the Despotic Power of Finance*. Kent, U.K.: Commonwealth Publishing.

Piketty, Thomas. 2014. *Capital in the Twenty-First Century*. Cambridge, Mass.: Harvard University Press.

Popper, Nathaniel. 2015. *Digital Gold: Bitcoin and the Inside Story of the Misfits and Millionaires Trying to Reinvent Money*. New York: HarperCollins.

Powers, Shawn M., and Michael Jablonski. 2015. *The Real Cyber War: The Political Economy of Internet Freedom*. Urbana: University of Illinois Press.

Puddington, Arch. 2013. "The Tea Party's Views on Tyranny, at Home and Abroad." Freedom at Issue (September 17). http:// freedomhouse.org/.

Reagan, Ronald. 1981. Inaugural Address (January 20). In *The American Presidency Project*, edited by Gerhard Peters and John T. Woolley. http://www.presidency.ucsb.edu/.

Redman, Jamie. 2015. "An Introduction to the Cypherpunk Tale." Bitcoin.com (August 30). http://www.bitcoin.com/.

——. 2016. "Central Banks' Failed Policies Are Strengthening Bitcoin." Bitcoin.com (January 12). https://news.bitcoin.com/.

Richardson, Tim. 2001. "Beenz Denies It's about to Be Canned: Global 'Net' Currency Devalued Big-Time." *The Register* (May 16). http:// www.theregister.co.uk/.

Rizzo, Pete. 2014a. "$100k Peter Thiel Fellowship Awarded to Ethereum's Vitalik Buterin." CoinDesk (June 5). http://www .coindesk.com/.

———. 2014b. "Tokyo Police Launch Investigation into Missing Mt. Gox Bitcoin." CoinDesk (July 30). http://www.coindesk.com/.

Robinson, Jeffrey. 2014. *Bitcon: The Naked Truth about Bitcoin.* Seattle: Amazon Digital Services.

"Ron Paul Sites Are Obsessed with Jews, Zionists, and Israel." 2011. RonPaulSupporters.com (December). http://ronpaulsupporters.com/.

Rothbard, Murray. 1974. *Egalitarianism as a Revolt against Nature and Other Essays.* Auburn, Ala.: Mises Institute, 2000.

———. 2002. *A History of Money and Banking in the United States: The Colonial Era to World War II.* Edited by Joseph Salerno. Auburn, Ala.: Mises Institute.

Sarkar, Debleena. 2015. "Mark Karpeles Faces New Charges in the Bitcoin Scandal." *International Business Times*, Australia ed. (August 3). http://www.ibtimes.com.au/.

Schneider, Nathan. 2014. "Meet Vitalik Buterin, the 20-Year-Old Who Is Decentralizing Everything." Shareable (July 31). http://www .shareable.net/.

Schroeder, Jeanne L. 2015. "Bitcoin and the Uniform Commercial Code." Cardozo Legal Studies Research Paper 458. http://papers.ssrn.com/.

Scott, Brett. 2014. "Visions of a Techno-Leviathan: The Politics of the Bitcoin Blockchain." *E-International Relations* (June). http://www .e-ir.info/.

———. 2016. "How Can Cryptocurrency and Blockchain Technology Play a Role in Building Social and Solidarity Finance?" United Nations Research Institute for Social Development Working Paper 2016-1. http://www.unrisd.org/.

Skocpol, Theda, and Vanessa Williamson. 2013. *The Tea Party and the Remaking of Republican Conservatism.* New York: Oxford University Press.

Shoff, Barbara. 2012. "Ron Paul Sound Currency Message Is Resonating with Worldwide Leaders, Including China." *PolicyMic* (October). http://mic.com/.

Shostak, Frank. 2013. "The Bitcoin Money Myth." Ludwig von Mises Institute (April). http://mises.org/.

Silverman, Jacob. 2013. "A Gun, a Printer, an Ideology." *New Yorker* (May). http://www.newyorker.com/.

Smart, Evander. 2015. "Why Bitcoin Qualifies as Money While the Dollar Is Just Currency." CryptoCoinsNews (May 4). http://www.cryptocoinsnews.com/.

Soltas, Evan. 2013. "Bitcoin Really Is an Existential Threat to the Modern Liberal State." *Bloomberg View* (April). http://www.bloombergview.com/.

Sorrentino, Nick. 2013. "Paul Krugman Is Scared: He Says 'Bitcoin Is Evil': Undermines Central Banks." Against Crony Capitalism (December 29). http://www.againstcronycapitalism.org/.

Suarez, Daniel. 2006. *Daemon*. New York: Dutton.

———. 2010. *Freedom*™. New York: Dutton.

Sutton, Anthony C. 1995. *The Federal Reserve Conspiracy*. San Diego: Dauphin Publications, 2014.

Swan, Melanie. 2015. *Blockchain: Blueprint for a New Economy*. Sebastopol, Calif.: O'Reilly Media.

Swanson, Tim. 2014. *The Anatomy of a Money-Like Informational Commodity: A Study of Bitcoin*. Seattle: Amazon Digital Services

Tapscott, Don, and Alex Tapscott. 2016. *Blockchain Revolution: How the Technology behind Bitcoin Is Changing Money, Business, and the World*. New York: Penguin.

Thierer, Adam, and Berin Szoka. 2009. "Cyber-Libertarianism: The Case for Real Internet Freedom." Technology Liberation Front (August 12). http://techliberation.com/.

Tkacz, Nathaniel. 2012. "From Open Source to Open Government: A Critique of Open Politics." *Ephemera: Theory and Politics in Organization* 12, no. 4: 386–405.

Tucker, Jeffrey A. 2015a. *Bit by Bit: How P2P Is Freeing the World*. Liberty.me.

———. 2015b. "A Theory of the Scam." Beautiful Anarchy (January 2). http://tucker.liberty.me/.

Turner, Fred. 2008. *From Counterculture to Cyberculture: Stewart Brand, the Whole Earth Network, and the Rise of Digital Utopianism*. Chicago: University of Chicago Press.

Tutino, Antonella, and Carlos E. J. M. Zarazaga. 2014. "Inflation Is Not Always and Everywhere a Monetary Phenomenon." *Economic Letter* (June). http://www.dallasfed.org/.

Varoufakis, Yanis. 2013. "Bitcoin and the Dangerous Fantasy of 'Apolitical' Money." Yanis Varoufakis (April 22). http://yanisvaroufakis.eu/.

Vigna, Paul, and Michael J. Casey. 2015. *The Age of Cryptocurrency: How Bitcoin and Digital Money Are Challenging the Global Economic Order*. New York: St. Martin's Press.

Weber, Max. 1919. "Politics as a Vocation." In Weber, *The Vocation Lectures: "Science as a Vocation," "Politics as a Vocation,"* 32–94. Indianapolis: Hackett, 2004.

Weiner, Keith. 2013. "Paul Krugman Is Wrong: Bitcoin Isn't Evil, but Monetary 'Stimulus' Is." *Forbes* (December). http://www.forbes .com/.

Welch, Robert. 1966. "The Truth in Time." *American Opinion* (November). http://www.ourrepubliconline.com/.

Wile, Rob. 2013. "927 People Own Half of All Bitcoins." *Business Insider* (December). http://www.businessinsider.com/.

Wilson, Matthew Graham, and Aaron Yelowitz. 2014. "Characteristics of Bitcoin Users: An Analysis of Google Search Data." Social Science Research Network (November 3). http://papers.ssrn.com/.

Winner, Langdon. 1997. "Cyberlibertarian Myths and the Prospects for Community." *ACM SIGCAS: Computers and Society* 27, no. 3: 14–19.

Wong, Joon Ian. 2014. "Venture Capital Funding for Bitcoin Startups Triples in 2014." CoinDesk (December 31). http://www.coin desk.com/.

Worstall, Tim. 2013. "Bitcoin Is More Like a Speculative Investment Than a Currency." *Forbes* (December 23). http://www.forbes.com/.

Yarow, Jay. 2013. "Tech People Are Passing around This Paul Krugman Quote on the Internet after He Called Bitcoin 'Evil.'" *Business Insider* (December 30). http://www.businessinsider.com/.

Yermack, David. 2014. "Is Bitcoin a Real Currency? An Economic Appraisal." Social Science Research Network (April). http://papers .ssrn.com/.

Zetter, Kim. 2009. "Bullion and Bandits: The Improbable Rise and Fall of E-Gold." *Wired* (June 9). http://www.wired.com/.

Zuesse, Eric. 2015. *Feudalism, Fascism, Libertarianism and Economics*. Bristol, UK: World Economics Association.

David Golumbia teaches in the English Department and the Media, Art, and Text PhD program at Virginia Commonwealth University. He is the author of *The Cultural Logic of Computation* and many articles on digital culture, language, and literary studies and theory, and he blogs on digital studies at http://uncomputing.org.